Tax Systems
of Western Europe

Third edition

Tax Systems of Western Europe

A guide for business and the professions

Third edition

C J PLATT

Gower

First published 1980. Second edition 1983. Third edition 1985

Published by

Gower Publishing Company Limited,
Gower House,
Croft Road,
Aldershot,
Hants GU11 3HR,
England

Gower Publishing Company,
Old Post Road,
Brookfield,
Vermont 05036,
U.S.A.

ISBN 0 566 02534 5

Gower Publishing Company Limited and the author have used their best efforts in collecting and preparing material for inclusion in *Tax Systems of Western Europe*. They do not assume, and hereby disclaim, any liability to any party for any loss or damage caused by errors or omissions in *Tax Systems of Western Europe*, whether such errors or omissions result from negligence, accident or any other cause.

British Library Cataloguing in Publication Data
Platt, C J
Tax Systems of Western Europe – 3rd ed.
1. Taxation – Law and legislation – Europe – Outlines, syllabi, etc. I. Title
LAW   343.404   84-18705
ISBN 0-566-02534-5   344.034

Typeset by FD Graphics Ltd., Fleet, Hampshire.
Printed in Great Britain by Dotesios (Printers) Limited, Bradford-on-Avon, Wiltshire.

CONTENTS

INTRODUCTION

Scope of the book

This book has been designed to provide summarised information on European tax systems. In addition to dealing with the taxation of income and capital gains by countries of Europe, including the United Kingdom, there is also some data on the general tax background of the countries concerned and an indication of sources of fuller and more detailed information on these subjects.

It is clear that, in a book of this size, the treatment of such a large subject can not be exhaustive, but in many cases reference is made to the existence of further provisions, which are not detailed in the book but which may be followed up by parties likely to be interested. It is hoped that what is lacking in completeness of coverage may be compensated for by the selection of matter of general interest and by the overall outline view provided.

In the third edition of this book all the material has been revised and updated in accordance with the latest information available at the time of going to press. It should however be appreciated that tax legislation and rates are continually changing, and that a check of the latest situation should therefore be made before taking a decision which is based on taxation considerations.

Countries covered

The following European countries, set out in alphabetical order, are covered in the book:

Austria	Greece	Netherlands
Belgium	Guernsey	Norway
Denmark	Republic of Ireland	Portugal
Finland	Isle of Man	Romania
France	Italy	Spain
Federal Republic	Jersey	Sweden
of Germany	Luxembourg	Switzerland
Gibraltar	Malta	United Kingdom

Introduction

There is a brief mention of Monaco (under France) and of Liechtenstein (under Switzerland).

Presentation of information

The information given starts with a short introduction to the tax environment of each country and the background against which its tax system operates, together with some of the main highlights of the system. Mention is often made, in connection with personal taxation, of the "progressiveness" of the taxes on income, meaning the extent to which the overall rate of tax increases at the higher levels of taxable income. Where taxes are progressive in impact, this is usually achieved by increasing rates on successive "slices" of taxable income, however large the total income, rather than by rates applied to the whole of the taxable income on a scale increasing with its size.

The main part of the material for each country is a summarised profile of the taxes on income and capital gains which are operative, the information being set out under a uniform scheme of headings, in order to facilitate reference and comparisons. Brief mention is made of any form of wealth tax, as this is often linked with taxes on income, but other taxes, such as those on turnover or value added, inheritance or capital transfer taxes and stamp duties are outside the purview of the book.

The explanatory notes and comments set out in the following paragraphs are given under the same headings as are used for the information on the taxes of each country.

Lists of taxes and legislation

References are made to the principal laws on which the taxes dealt with are based. In most cases the original legislation has been amended by subsequent laws. Even in respects where the basic law is not changed, rates of taxation and the amounts of allowances are liable to be settled or altered by subsidiary legislation, such as the Finance Acts in the United Kingdom. In some countries there are separate regulations dealing with the detailed application of the law. In most countries there is no regular codification or consolidation of the complete law on the subject.

In some countries there are local as well as national taxes, and usually the rates of any local taxes, and in some cases the regulations for their application, vary in the different areas of the country. It is not feasible to give information on all the local variations, but an indication is given of the general nature of the taxes and, where possible, the range of rates. A brief note is also given of the scope of any form of wealth tax which is in operation. The rest of the details in the summaries deal only with the national taxes on income and capital gains. Any major change in the tax system recently made, such as the adoption of a tax imputation system, is noted either under this heading or elsewhere in the summary.

Individuals' taxation
Companies and other associations are usually subject in general to the same basic regulations as individuals for the computation of taxes, so far as they are applicable, but important modifications affecting companies are set out under the later headings dealing with their taxation. There are usually different tax-rate scales for individuals and companies.

(a) Income charged
Under this heading details are given of the general scope of the taxes on the income and gains of resident and non-resident individuals respectively. "Residence" is usually, but not always, defined in the tax laws of the country. The definition in some cases is quite simple (such as living in the country for more than half the tax year) but in other cases it is more involved. Both "residence" and "domicile" are matters of legal interpretation which must be applied under individual circumstances and it is not possible to set out the full conditions in this book. In most countries "residents" are liable for the taxes of the country on income from all sources, whereas "non-residents" are liable only on income arising in the country, but some countries, such as Switzerland, apply a system of territoriality. This means that a resident is not liable for Swiss taxes on income from real property or a permanent establishment outside Switzerland. Some countries have special provisions for the taxation of temporary residents.

(b) Year and basis of assessment
The tax year adopted is shown (e.g. a year corresponding

with the calendar year) and also the general basis of assessment used (e.g. the chargeable income of the preceding year). Profits of businesses are usually assessed on the basis of their accounting period ending in the relevant year. Mention is made under this heading of any arrangements for provisional or instalment payments of tax to be made pending assessment of the final liability: when such payments are required, they are usually a proportion of the liability of the previous year.

(c) Computation of taxable income

The information given under this heading starts with a general summary of the overall basis of computation which is adopted for individuals before dealing with the various categories of taxable income. Some countries have a "schedular" system, under which different types of income are assessed under separate schedules with differing regulations and sometimes subject to different rates of tax. Other countries aggregate the various types of taxable income and, after making any admissible deductions, apply a single scale of tax to the net total. Details are given for each country of the treatment for assessment purposes of married persons and of partnerships.

Taxable income is dealt with under the following categories:

(i) Business or professional income

Details are given of the general method of computation adopted, including admissible capital allowances. Mention is also made under this heading of the availability of any special tax incentives, such as accelerated depreciation, intended to encourage development and capital investment.

(ii) Capital gains

Particulars are given of types of capital gain which are treated as taxable or which are specifically exempted, and of any special conditions attached. Unless chargeable capital gains are aggregated with other income, the rate of tax applied is quoted.

(iii) Special trades

In a number of countries certain types of business undertaking, such as agriculture, insurance, shipping or air transport, have special treatment for tax purposes. The main types of undertaking which are subject to such regulations are listed.

(iv) Salaries, wages etc. and pensions

Any special provisions relating to the assessment of remuneration from employment or former employment and benefits in kind are quoted and particulars are given of any deductible expense allowances. Most countries provide for a number of exemptions, as for instance for the emoluments of foreign diplomatic representatives or for some kinds of pension, but it is not feasible to quote these in full. Mention is made of any arrangements for the deduction of tax at source.

(v) Dividends, interest etc.

The deductibility of tax at source from dividends and other distributions by resident companies, and also from interest payments, is dealt with, as is the availability of tax credits under an imputation system. Some countries treat dividends, interest, royalties and other income under one heading as income from capital. In some cases tax deducted at source from dividends is a true withholding tax, the amounts deducted being handed over to the revenue authorities: in such cases the tax is treated either as a final withholding tax in settlement of the liability on the income in question, or as a payment on account, for which credit is given in the computation of the taxpayer's overall liability. In other cases, the tax is not one payable by the company in addition to that chargeable on its profits but is merely a means of arriving at a net amount payable to shareholders out of its profits after tax, and the amount 'deducted' is not a true withholding tax.

(vi) Income from letting and leasing

The taxability of rents and other income from property and, where it applies, of the rental value of owner-occupied property, is dealt with.

(vii) Other income

Brief details are given of taxable income which is not included under any of the headings above, such as royalties in many cases.

Introduction

(d) Deductions from total income

Admissible deductions, insofar as they have not been taken from any of the separate categories of income of individuals referred to under (c) above, are dealt with under the following headings:

(i) **General deductions:** i.e. such as interest payments, insurance or pensions contributions and losses brought forward.

(ii) **Personal and other allowances:** including married and single allowances and reliefs for earned income, children and other dependants, age or disability. Such reliefs are sometimes given in the form of tax rebates rather than as deductions from taxable income.

(iii) **Tax credits:** under tax imputation systems or double taxation agreements, and where tax has been suffered by deduction at source.

(e) Tax deducted at source

Reference is made to types of income mentioned in earlier paragraphs from which tax is deducted at source, either in general or only from payments to non-residents. Some deductions give rise to tax credits against subsequent assessments, while others are withholding taxes taken in final satisfaction of the tax liability on the income in question.

Companies' taxation

The provisions for the taxation of the profits of companies etc., insofar as they differ from those which are applicable to individuals, are dealt with under the headings which follow.

(a) Types of undertaking charged

The types of undertakings charged under the regulations applicable to companies are indicated: these commonly include various kinds of company registered under the laws of the home country, resident branches of foreign companies and other associations such as limited partnerships or co-operatives, all of which may be charged under these regulations rather than those for individuals.

(b) Income charged
The chargeability of the profits or income of resident and
non-resident companies respectively are stated and these are
usually subject to the same distinctions as apply in the case of
individuals. The criteria laid down for "residence" in the
country in the case of a company are usually quoted.

(c) Computation of taxable income
The computation of the taxable income of companies is
generally in most respects in accordance with the same rules
as for individuals, with some obvious exceptions where these
are applicable only to individuals (e.g. as regards personal
reliefs). Points of difference in the case of companies arise,
for instance, in the treatment of inter-company dividends
(which may be exempt from tax), the company's own dividend distributions (which are in some countries admissible
deductions in arriving at the company's assessable income)
and capital gains (which may all be included in ordinary
taxable income although certain corresponding gains made
by individuals are exempt and others are separately taxed).
The principal features of this sort are mentioned in the
summary for each country.

Double taxation agreements
Nearly all countries have some treaties with other countries for
the relief of double taxation. In the summary for each country
the approximate number of full agreements which are in operation is mentioned, but the numbers change from year to year. In
addition, there are often restricted agreements, dealing for
instance only with shipping and air transport revenues, and
many countries give some form of unilateral relief for double
taxation, referred to in the summaries, in cases which are not
covered by a tax treaty.

In all cases where reference is made to a provision for the
deduction of tax at source from the payment of a particular kind
of income, it should be noted that the provisions may well be
modified as regards payments made to a non-resident with whose
country a double taxation agreement is in force.

Introduction

Rates of tax

In order to give an approximate indication of the rates of tax in each country, in some of which changes occur quite frequently, the latest information available at the time of writing as to standard rates of national taxes on the income of individuals and companies is set out, together with some sample figures from any graduated scale of tax and the principal personal reliefs. The rates of local and other special taxes, wealth tax and capital gains tax are usually given as part of the text matter dealing with those taxes. A separate summary is included showing the general rates of withholding taxes deducted from payments to non-resident companies of dividends, interest and royalties and also the rates which are applied to such income under the terms of any double taxation agreement with the United Kingdom. The rates of withholding tax on payments to individuals are not always the same as for companies.

SOURCES OF INFORMATION

The comments which follow on other sources of information on the income taxes of European countries refer only to information available in the English language. The sources quoted are such as will provide in most cases information in much greater detail than is possible in a book of this size dealing with a number of different countries.

General information

Apart from the specific sources mentioned later, some more general methods of obtaining information may be referred to.

1. Firms of accountants. Firms of professional accountants can undoubtedly help. One which is part of a large international firm may be able to give access to some of the publications referred to later and will be able to provide detailed information about the taxation situation in overseas countries in which the firm has an office: in addition such firms usually have taxation experts who can deal with questions arising in other areas. International firms will be helpful on such matters as the tax situation of foreign branches, employees working overseas and withholding taxes on income from other countries. A firm which has domestic interests only will normally have contacts with one of the international firms to whom an introduction can be given.

2. Tax consultants. A number of practising tax consultants specialise in advising clients on arranging their affairs in such a way as to minimise their tax liabilities. Tax consultants in the United Kingdom who are listed in, for instance, the "Yellow Pages" of the London telephone directory, are largely concerned with problems of UK taxation, but they may be expected also to have information on the tax advantages or disadvantages of investing funds or carrying on business in particular overseas countries.

3. Foreign embassies, legations and consulates. It may be worth consulting the most conveniently accessible representative in your home country of the foreign country in which you are interested. The commercial department of an embassy or legation may be able to give some useful information and will no doubt be aware of any official publications dealing with the taxation of their country which are available in a language understood by the enquirer.

4. Libraries. Specialist libraries are likely to have available some of the publications referred to later in this section or others dealing with certain individual countries. In addition they will probably have on their shelves general publications which may be helpful on such matters as double taxation agreements or the "tax haven" advantages of other countries, on both of which a good deal has been written. Big cities may have a specialist library of this nature. In London, instances which may be mentioned are:

(a) The library of the Inland Revenue at Somerset House, London WC2, which has an extensive range of material on the tax laws and regulations of foreign countries (much of it in the language of origin) which may be used with permission.

(b) The libraries of the professional accounting bodies, which are normally only available for use by their own members, e.g. the Institute of Chartered Accountants in England and Wales in Moorgate Place, London EC2.

(c) The City Business Library in London Wall, London EC2.

The librarian of a local library can no doubt say where the nearest library likely to have the necessary facilities is to be found.

Introduction

5. *United Kingdom taxation.* At the offices of all H.M. Inspectors of Taxes in the United Kingdom there are available free of charge a large number of explanatory pamphlets dealing with different aspects of UK taxation, which are certain to be authoritative and up to date. Advice on specific matters of doubt can also be obtained from such offices.

Specific publications

Some more specific English language publications dealing with taxation in various countries are detailed below.

1. Publications edited and compiled by direction of the Board of Inland Revenue of the United Kingdom:

(a) The series of country booklets "Income taxes outside the United Kingdom" each of which comprises a fairly detailed summary of the regulations dealing with the taxation of income in the country concerned, based on the latest information available at the time of issue. The booklets are based on the original texts of legislation or reliable translations, and the information is presented under a standard scheme of headings throughout the series.

   The most recent of the present booklets were issued in 1980 and the editions for most countries are earlier than this, though the information is in many cases brought up to date in the "Overseas tax development notes" mentioned at (b) below: at least two new booklets are planned and should be available in due course. The dates of the latest editions at present available are shown in the tabulated summary of publications on individual countries at the end of the introduction.

(b) "Overseas tax development notes", published at intervals through the year, provide an updating service for the information contained in the booklets of the "Income taxes outside the United Kingdom" series. The notes, which are referenced to the country booklets, give the latest available information on important new legislation and also include annual summaries of company tax rates and of rates of withholding taxes on dividends, interest and patent royalties in over 100 countries.

   The "Overseas tax development notes" are available by

annual subscription from the Board of Inland Revenue, Foreign Intelligence Section, Room 11, Somerset House, London WC2: copies are also usually held by libraries which have the country booklets.

2. Several of the large international firms of Chartered Accountants publish individual booklets on various countries throughout the world in which they have offices. Apart from general information likely to be useful to a business concern which is considering establishing itself in an overseas country or intending to have dealings with it, the booklets contain a fairly comprehensive summary of the principal features of the tax system of the country. These booklets are not generally available for sale, being specifically designed for the staff and clients of the firms issuing them. They may however in some cases be made available on request to persons other than clients. Some of the booklets which were issued some years ago have not been updated.

3. Deloitte, Haskins & Sells, one of the large international firms of Chartered Accountants, issues an "International Tax and Business Service" dealing with a number of countries. This is in loose-leaf form, regularly updated, and gives very full information on income and other taxes for individuals and companies (systems, computation, rates, withholding taxes, special problems, tax treaties etc.). There is a separate volume on tax matters affecting US citizens abroad. This firm also published "Taxation in Europe 1983", giving an outline of the tax systems in operation at 1st January 1983 of a number of countries, including those dealt with in this book.

4. The International Bureau of Fiscal Documentation of Amsterdam publishes in English a "European Taxation" service. This consists of (a) a monthly journal containing articles and notes on current developments, (b) a supplementary service consisting of regularly updated summaries dealing with tax treaties and other matters and (c) guides to European taxation, summarising company tax legislation and rates, individual taxation, taxes on investment income etc. in a number of countries, with regular updating of information. This is a most comprehensive and detailed service but it is unlikely that individuals other than international tax specialists would normally subscribe for it. Copies may however be available for consultation in the types of specialist library mentioned earlier in this section and in the libraries of firms of accountants with international practices.

5. Several well established annual tax guides for the United Kingdom are published which give a large amount of detail, kept fully up to date, and quote relevant case law. These include the guides published by Tolley Publishing Co Ltd on income tax, corporation tax and capital gains taxes, and Rowlands tax guide published by Butterworth & Co (Publishers) Ltd. Tolley also publish similar guides on taxation in the Republic of Ireland, Gibraltar, the Channel Islands and the Isle of Man. The Institute of Chartered Accountants in England and Wales publish, among other works on United Kingdom taxation, the regularly updated "Chartac Taxation Manual". Other authoritative works of greater length than some of the above on all aspects of United Kingdom taxation are of course also available.

Summary of specific publications

The publications mentioned above are no more than a selection from a large list. It is however believed that they are all of a kind likely to give authoritative and reasonably up to date information, though not necessarily in great depth. These and certain other publications briefly described below are included in the summary which follows and which indicates the countries covered by the various sources. The dates show the most recent year dealt with in the latest available edition: for those which are regularly updated on a loose-leaf system or by annual editions, no date is shown.

These sources are:

1. Inland Revenue
   Booklets in the series "Income taxes outside the United Kingdom" referred to above.

2. European Taxation
   The guides to European taxation, included in the supplementary service dealing with individual countries, referred to above.

3. Arthur Andersen & Co.

4. Peat, Marwick, Mitchell & Co.
5. Price Waterhouse & Co.
6. Touche Ross & Co.
7. Spicer & Oppenheim
   Large international firms of Chartered Accountants whose
   guides, referred to above, cover a number of different countries. Other countries are covered, but any editions issued
   before 1979 are omitted from this summary. Peat, Marwick,
   Mitchell & Co. also published a book "European Taxation
   1981" giving an outline of the tax systems in operation at the
   end of 1980 of the more important commercial countries of
   Western Europe.

8. Deloitte, Haskins & Sells
   The loose-leaf taxation service referred to above.

9. Tolley Publishing Co. Ltd.
   The tax guides referred to above.

10. Tax Management Inc.
   A division of The Bureau of National Affairs of Washington
   USA: a loose-leaf service on business operations in various
   countries is published, in which an extensive and regularly
   updated section on taxation is included.

11. Matthew Bender (USA)
   "Foreign Tax and Trade Briefs" are published in New York
   as a loose-leaf service which is regularly updated. The main
   tax features and rates are summarised for most countries
   other than those of Eastern Europe.

Publications on individual countries

	INLAND REVENUE	EUROPEAN TAXATION	ARTHUR ANDERSEN	PEAT, MARWICK, MITCHELL	PRICE WATERHOUSE	TOUCHE ROSS	SPICER & OPPENHEIM	DELOITTE, HASKINS & SELLS	TOLLEY	TAX MANAGEMENT	BENDER
	1.	2.	3.	4.	5.	6.	7.	8.	9.	10.	11.
Austria	'78	+			'81	'79		+		+	+
Belgium	'77	+			'82			+			+
Denmark	'76	+	'79		'82		'80			+	+
Finland		+	'79			'80					+
France	'76	+		'80	'79	'79		+		+	+
Germany*	'79	+		'80	'83			+		+	+
Gibraltar	'79						'80		+		
Greece	**	+								+	+
Guernsey	'78	+		'82	'81		'81		+		+
Ireland	'77	+	'79	'83	'81	'81	'83	+	+	+	+
Isle of Man	'79	+							+		
Italy	'77	+			'83	'83	'82	+		+	+
Jersey	'78	+		'82	'81				+		+
Luxembourg	'78	+			'82	'81				+	+
Malta	'79				'82						
Netherlands	'79	+		'80	'80			+		+	+
Norway	'80	+	'79	'82							+
Portugal	'78	+			'81						+
Romania	'76	+			'82						
Spain	'79	+		'80	'82	'82		+		+	+
Sweden	**	+	'79			'79	'80			+	+
Switzerland***		+			'81	'83	'83	+		+	+
United Kingdom		+		'82	'83			+	+	+	+

*Commerce Clearing House (USA) publish a detailed work on Germany in a World Tax Series.

**Booklet in preparation.

***Coopers & Lybrand AG published a booklet "Taxation in Switzerland" 1982.

Countries of Eastern Europe

This book does not deal with taxation in countries of Eastern Europe, other than Romania, but it may be noted that the "European Taxation" supplementary services referred to above include cover on Czechoslovakia, German Democratic Republic, Poland and USSR and that Price Waterhouse & Co include in their series a volume on Eastern Europe, covering Albania, Bulgaria, Czechoslovakia, German Democratic Republic, Hungary, Poland, Romania, USSR and Yugoslavia.

AUSTRIA

Austria is a constitutional federal democracy, made up of nine provinces. The tax system has a number of features similar to that of West Germany and is based on income tax and corporation tax. There is also a business tax on the income of businesses, used for federal and local purposes, and a wealth tax payable by individuals and companies. Income tax on income from employment, from investments and from royalties is deducted at source, and there is a separate additional tax on directors' fees received from Austrian companies.

The rates of personal taxation are quite high but the tax threshold is raised, and the effective rates are lowered, by the system of giving the various personal reliefs in the form of tax credits rather than by reducing taxable income. Tax is on a progressive scale but the top rate is only reached at a very high level of income. Capital gains on business assets are included in taxable business income and other short-term gains are taxed as speculative transactions. Gains on longer-term investments, not held as assets of a business, are exempt except in some cases where they arise on disposal of a substantial interest in a company.

There are a number of tax incentives encouraging business investment, including:

(i) Up to 25% of profit before tax may be taken to an investment reserve for the acquisition of depreciable business assets, its use for this purpose being subject to a number of prescribed conditions.

(ii) Accelerated depreciation rates are available, restricted to expenditure calculated after deducting any amounts used from investment reserve.

(iii) Individuals may make transfers from business profits to tax-free reserves which can be capitalised after five years.

(iv) An investment allowance on the cost of depreciable assets for use in a business in Austria is given on expenditure incurred, after deducting any investment reserve used for this purpose and any costs on which accelerated depreciation is claimed.

1

Austria

1 LIST OF TAXES

(a) Taxes on income
   (i) Income Tax *(Einkommensteuer):*
      on the income of individuals, discharged in part by deductions at source for:
        Wages tax *(Lohnsteuer)*
        Capital yields tax *(Kapitalertragsteuer)*
   (ii) Directors' Remuneration Tax *(Aufsichtsratsabgabe)*
   (iii) Corporation Tax *(Körperschaftsteuer):*
      on the profits of companies and other entities.
   (iv) Tax on Interest *(Zinsertragsteuer)*

(b) Other taxes (not further referred to in this summary)
   (i) Business Tax *(Gewerbesteuer):*
      levied on business undertakings for federal and local purposes: basic rate on business income is 5% but other elements and municipal surcharges raise the effective rate to an average of 15%. Business tax for the year is a deductible expense in computing net profits for income tax and corporation tax.
   (ii) Wealth Tax *(Vermögensteuer):*
      a federal tax payable by resident individuals and companies on net worldwide wealth, and by others on net wealth in Austria at a rate of 1%, subject to personal and dependants' allowances for resident individuals. A 10% reduction in the tax on business property is proposed in the 1984 Budget.

2 LEGISLATION

The basic laws, subject to subsequent amendments, are:
   Income Tax Law of 24 November 1972
   Directors' Remuneration Tax Law of 28 March 1934
   Corporation Tax Law of 6 July 1966.
   Tax on Interest Law of 29 November 1983.
Detailed effect is given by ministerial decree.

3 INCOME TAX – INDIVIDUALS

(a) Income charged
   Residents and persons employed in Austria under work permit or contract for at least six months: Total income

from all sources
Other persons: Income arising in Austria

(b) *Year and basis of assessment*
Industrial, commercial, professional and agricultural activities:
Accounting period ending in the tax year (calendar year)
Other activities: Tax year

(c) *Computation of taxable income*
Tax is assessed under a number of separate categories on the individual income of each taxpayer (including married persons). Members of ordinary partnerships are individually liable for income tax on their shares of the profits.

(i) **Business income:**
Basis
Profits and gains from all the assets (other than land) used for industrial, commercial etc. activities and for agriculture are assessable, the liability being normally computed by comparison of balance sheets for successive accounting periods, but may be determined on the basis of business income less necessary expenses if proper accounts are not kept: there are rules for the valuation of assets which are normally valued at cost less depreciation, but valuation on a going concern basis may be used if lower. Some details of available tax incentives are given in the introductory material on page 1.
Depreciation allowances
Prescribed rates are laid down, accelerated depreciation being permitted in certain cases: small amounts may be written off in full: depletion basis is used for mines etc.

(ii) **Capital gains:**
Business assets
Gains are normally included in business income, with certain exceptions on sale or cessation of business.
Investments
Gains are assessable in certain cases where a substantial interest is held, but at half the normal rate of tax and there are some exemptions: otherwise they are exempt,

except when included in business assets or in "speculative transactions" – see below.

Speculative transactions

Gains on sale of real property held for less than 5 years and other assets less than one year are assessable as ordinary income, subject to certain exemptions.

(iii) Professional income

Profits of professions and other independent work may be computed much as those derived from businesses but a cash basis is frequently used for computing income.

(iv) Salaries, wages etc., pensions:

Income from employment and former employment is assessable, subject to exemptions (e.g. rental of house provided up to prescribed limit, welfare etc. benefits) and a minimum flat rate deduction of 4,914 S. for costs: non-resident employees whose income is subject to wages tax are taxed at a flat rate 10% (up to 3,120 S. per month) or 20% (on higher amounts) with no deductions for costs: certain fees etc. bear a final withholding tax at 20% only. Directors' fees from Austrian companies bear a directors' remuneration tax of 30% (increased in the 1984 Budget to 45%), deducted in arriving at taxable income for income tax purposes. Wages tax and directors' remuneration tax are deducted at source from income which is reduced by an employee's credit of 4,000 S.

(v) Dividends, interest etc.

Income from movable capital, subject to exemption of interest up to 7,000 S. on Austrian bank deposits and after deducting expenses, is charged capital yields tax at 20%, deducted at source: for non-residents this is normally a final withholding tax. As from the beginning of 1984, an additional tax of 7½% is payable on interest on bank deposits and bonds, deducted at source.

(vi) Income from letting and leasing

Income less expenses from real property, leasing movable assets and from royalties is assessed under this heading.

(vii) Other income

Miscellaneous receipts less expenses (e.g. from royalties,

annuities or occasional commissions): capital yields tax is withheld at source from royalties.

(d) Deductions from total income
(i) General deductions
Special expenses and contributions, e.g. annuities, payments in connection with building of houses, unrecouped independent business losses (which may be carried forward for up to 5 years), insurance premiums. A minimum annual deduction of 3,276 S. is allowed for such expenses.

(ii) Personal and other allowances
Personal allowance, sole wage-earner's (married taxpayer), employee's or pensioner's credit are amongst the reliefs granted to residents by way of tax credits. Child allowances have been replaced by tax-free child subsidies.

(iii) Tax credits
Tax deducted at source and reliefs as at (ii) above are available for credit against the total liability of residents.

(e) Tax deducted at source
(i) Wages tax and directors' remuneration tax: see (c) (iv) above.

(ii) Capital yields tax: see (c) (v) and (vii) above.

(iii) Additional tax on interest: see (c) (v) above.

4   CORPORATION TAX – COMPANIES ETC.

(a) Types of undertaking charged
Public limited companies *(Aktiengesellschaften – abbreviation AG)*
Private limited companies *(Gesellschaften mit beschränkter Haftung – abbreviation GmbH)*
Co-operative societies
(For partnerships, see 3.(c) above).

(b) Income charged
Resident companies etc. (i.e. whose business, management or registered office is in Austria): Income from all sources

Non-resident companies etc.: Profits from undertakings carried on in Austria (tax on dividends, interest etc., royalties and fees satisfied by tax deducted at source – see 3.(e) above).

(c) *Computation of taxable income*
Corporation tax is computed in the main in accordance with the rules applicable to individuals' income tax. Dividends from a company in which an interest of 25% or more is held are excluded from taxable profits. Most capital gains are taxed as business income.

5 DOUBLE TAXATION AGREEMENTS

Comprehensive agreements are in force between Austria and the United Kingdom and also over 30 other countries.

6 RATES OF TAX

The rates of tax are subject to change from year to year, but the samples shown below for income of 1983 give some indication of recent rates. Amounts are stated in Schillings (S.).

(a) *Individuals' income tax*
Rates of tax on successive slices of taxable income rise from 21% on the first 50,000 S. to 45% on 200,001 – 250,000 S. and 62% on over 1,500,000 S.
Allowances include tax credits as follows:
Personal   5,100 S.
Sole wage-earner   3,900 S. (married taxpayer with spouse whose earned income does not exceed 10,000S.)
Employee's credit   4,000 S.
Pensioner's credit   2,400 S.

(b) *Companies etc. – corporation tax*
Basic rates on total taxable income:
Rising in stages from 30% on up to 200,000 S. to 50% on 500,101 – 1,000,000 S. and 55% on over 1,142,800 S.
Reduced rates: on distributed profits of resident joint stock companies: 50% of basic rate.

(c) Withholding taxes
Payments to non-resident companies:

	General rate	Rate applied under UK double taxation agreement
Dividends	20%	10% or 15%*
Interest (convertible and profit-sharing bonds only)	20%	NIL
Royalties	20%	NIL

*Lower rate to a company owning 25% or more of voting power.

BELGIUM

Belgium, a relatively small but very densely populated country, maintains a high standard of living in spite of having to import most of its raw materials. As a natural consequence, the country is highly export-oriented and also encourages foreign investment.

Tax incentives are available for new investments in fixed assets, particularly any in development areas or made by exporters, and also for dividends on newly-issued stocks in their first five years. There are special tax concessions for non-Belgian employees who are only in the country on a temporary basis.

There is a highly progressive scale of personal taxation, but the top rates are only reached at very high income levels and there is a limit to total tax set at 67½% of taxable income for residents and 71.55% for non-residents, who are liable for a 6% additional surcharge on their tax.

Capital gains on sale of business assets are included in taxable business income, but certain personal gains realised by individuals are exempt.

Investment incentives now consist mainly of deductions from the cost of investments in new business assets, with special rates for scientific research and energy-saving investments. In addition, a number of enterprise zones have been created where certain kinds of high technology concerns are guaranteed tax exemptions for 10 years.

Belgium has a large number of double taxation agreements with other countries. There is a system of withholding taxes on payments to non-residents of dividends, interest, royalties and annuities.

1 LIST OF TAXES AND LEGISLATION

(a) Income tax

The basic Income Tax Code was co-ordinated by Royal Decree of 26 February 1964, subsequently amended. Four main categories of taxpayer are distinguished:

Individual income tax *(impôt des personnes physiques)* levied on resident individuals

Non-residents income tax *(impôt des non-résidents)* levied on non-resident individuals and corporations

Corporate income tax *(impôt des sociétés)* levied on resident companies etc.

Non-profit making organisations income tax *(impôt des personnes morales)* levied on resident legal entities.

(b) Local taxes (not further dealt with in this summary)

Levied by municipalities and provinces, include surcharges of up to 6% on the income tax.

2 INCOME TAX – INDIVIDUALS

(a) Income charged

Residents: Income from all sources
Non-residents: Income from Belgian sources.

(b) Year and basis of assessment

The tax year is the calendar year: taxable income generally is that of the previous calendar year or accounting period ending within that year. Advance payments of tax are required in many cases, often through the medium of deductions at source.

(c) Computation of taxable income

Tax is calculated on the total joint income of husband and wife subject to certain reliefs. Partnerships are normally taxed as "companies", but see 3(a) below.

(i) Business or "professional" income:

Basis

Net profit from agricultural, manufacturing or trading activities (in which is included associated income from real property or investments) after deduction of business expenses and losses: there are rules dealing with admissible expenses and valuation of stocks. Unrecovered losses may be carried forward for up to 5 years.

Depreciation allowances

Rates for various types of asset including goodwill are subject to agreement between the taxpayer and the tax authorities and accelerated depreciation and tax-free investment reserves have been available for certain assets.

As from 1983, free depreciation and tax-free investment reserves have been replaced by direct investment deductions from the cost of investment in new business assets, with higher deductions from scientific research and energy-saving investments.

(ii) Capital gains:

Business assets

Gains are included in taxable business income, but, if assets held for more than 5 years, they are partially exempt and are taxed at a reduced rate.

Undeveloped land

Gains are taxed if realised within 8 years of acquisition.

Substantial shareholdings

Gains are taxable in some cases.

Speculations

Gains may be taxed separately as miscellaneous income.

Exempt gains

Gains from other sources (including in some cases those arising on transfer of a business) are exempt.

(iii) Salaries, wages etc., professional income

Income from employment, former employment and self-employment in professional activities is taxable with business profits as "professional" income: standard rates of deduction from earned income (maximum 75,000 fr.) for expenses may be claimed instead of actual expenses: from the income year 1984, the maximum standard deduction is increased to 125,000 fr. There is also an earned income deduction of 10,000 fr. and a working wife's deduction of 56,000 fr. Income from employment is subject to a payroll withholding tax.

From 1984, employees are entitled to certain deductions from taxable income for the purchase price of shares in their employer's company.

(iv) Dividends, interest etc.

Dividends and interest are subject to a withholding tax of 20%, which is available for tax credit, and dividends from Belgian sources carry an additional tax credit in respect of corporate income tax: royalties, annuities etc. to residents are exempt from the withholding tax. Certain dividends on newly-issued shares may be exempt (see 3(c) below). The rate of withholding tax is increased to 25% from 1984 income.

(v) Income from letting and leasing

Taxable income from real property is based on an official valuation in the property register: the notional income is increased for a property used for business purposes and is reduced for an owner-occupied dwelling house. There is a system of advance payments for which tax credit is given against the total tax liability.

(vi) Other income

Miscellaneous taxable income includes payments received under maintenance agreements and subsidies from public funds less necessary expenses. "Speculative" gains are separately taxed at 33%.

(d) Deductions from total income

(i) General deductions

Permitted deductions include losses brought forward, interest on loans in connection with real or movable property, charitable etc. donations and 80% of payments under maintenance agreements.

(ii) Personal and other allowances

Deductions for dependants are given in the form of tax credits. Allowances from earned income are given as shown at (c) (iii) above.

(iii) Tax credits
Credit is given for advance payments of tax, for the allowances mentioned at (ii) above and, in certain cases, for foreign tax suffered.

(e) Tax deducted at source

(i) Employment income: see (c) (iii) above.

(ii) Dividends, interest etc.: see (c) (iv) above.

3 INCOME TAX – COMPANIES ETC.

(a) Types of undertaking charged
Public limited companies *(sociétés anonymes, "SA")*
Private limited companies *(sociétés de personnes à responsabilité limitée, "SARL")*
Partnerships and other associations
Private limited companies, ordinary partnerships and some other associations may under certain conditions opt for assessment as individuals in the names of the partners or members.

(b) Income charged
Resident companies etc. (i.e. those having their principal establishment or centre of administration in Belgium): Income from all sources
Non-resident companies etc.: Income from Belgian sources

(c) Computation of taxable income
Tax is chargeable on the income of the accounting year ending in the previous calendar year. The computation is in the main as for the income tax on individuals (see 2.(c) above) but with some modifications. Dividends received by one resident company from another are however 95% exempt from tax (90% if the recipient is an investment company). Dividends paid on newly-issued stock are deductible in assessing profits for the first 5 years and for this period are exempt in the hands of shareholders.

4 DOUBLE TAXATION AGREEMENTS

There are comprehensive agreements in force between Belgium and the United Kingdom and also over 30 other countries. A credit for foreign tax on movable capital and some other miscellaneous income may be given at 15% of the foreign income.

5 RATES OF TAX

The rates of tax are subject to change from year to year, but the samples shown below for income of 1983 give some indication of recent rates. Amounts are stated in Belgian francs (fr.).

(a) Individual income tax
For taxable incomes up to 750,000 fr. official tables show chargeable tax for various totals of income before any reduction for dependants. The taxpayer for instance with no dependants and the full 750,000 fr. income is liable for tax of 252,500 fr.
On successive slices of income thereafter rates of tax range from 47.5% on 750,001–1,000,000 fr. to 72% on the amount over 4,000,000 fr. There is an additional surcharge of 6% for non-residents. The total tax is however limited to 67.5% of total taxable income for residents and 71.55% (67.5% + 6%) for non-residents.
Allowances are given in the form of tax credits for a spouse (standard allowance 4,618 fr.) and for dependent children ranging from 5% of tax plus 500 fr. for one child (maximum 5,118 fr.) to 147,788 fr. for more than 6: the rates of allowance are increased from 1984.

(b) Corporate income tax
Standard rate (Belgian companies): 45%
Reduced rates: for taxable income less than 14,400,000 fr. (but, from 1984, only if distributions do not exceed 13% of paid-up share capital and issue premiums) and for some kinds of capital gain.
Non-resident companies: 50%

Belgium

(c) Withholding taxes

Payments to non-resident companies:

	General rate	Rate applied under UK double taxation agreement
Dividends	20%*	15%
Interest	20%*	15%
Royalties	20%	NIL

* Increased to 25% from 1984 income.

DENMARK

Denmark became a member of the EEC at the same time as the United Kingdom. The country relies much on exports of farm produce. Personal national income tax is not at a very heavy rate, nor is the scale of rates steeply progressive, but the communal and other local taxes on income, as well as several special purpose taxes, increase the total burden on individuals considerably. There is however an overall limit to the amount of tax paid by an individual, based on a proportion of income. In addition, there is an annual wealth tax and value added tax was introduced in 1977. Capital gains arising from a business are in general included in taxable business income, but for individuals special income tax is chargeable on certain other gains and lump-sum receipts.

There is provision for generous depreciation allowances on plant etc., at up to 30% (at the taxpayer's option) on the reducing balance adjusted from 1982 for inflation, based on the consumer price index. Tax incentives are available for developments in the less populated areas of the country under the Regional Development Act 1972. A temporary investment allowance was introduced for purchases of plant, equipment etc. (other than motor cars) in the years 1981 to 1983. Tax-free allocations to an investment reserve are also permitted for corporations under certain circumstances. Temporary residents, for up to three years, are allowed special tax concessions.

A tax imputation system was introduced in 1979/80, prior to which a final withholding tax was deducted from dividends. Interest and royalties paid to non-residents are exempt from tax. Double taxation agreements are in force with a large number of countries and unilateral relief is also available. The Danish tax laws do not apply in the Faroe Islands or Greenland.

Denmark

1   LIST OF TAXES AND LEGISLATION

The basic legislation consists of the laws quoted below, as subsequently amended.

(a) Individuals

(i)   **National Income Tax** *(Indkomstskat til staten):* Charged on total income (National Tax Law No. 149 of 10th April 1922 and Tax at Source Law of 31st March 1967).

(ii) **Special Income Tax** *(Saerlig indkomstskat):* Charged on certain capital gains and lump-sum payments (Law No. 454 of 19th July 1977).

The following taxes are not further dealt with in this summary:

(iii) **Local taxes**
Communal and county income taxes and church tax (all based on income as assessed for national income tax) are levied at rates varying in the different districts, currently at between about 18% and 30% in total (e.g. Copenhagen 29.4%): for non-residents there is a fixed rate of 20%.

(iv) **Capital Tax** *(Formueskat til staten):*
A wealth tax computed on capital assets other than personal chattels, furniture etc.: non-residents receiving income from employment or with a business or property in Denmark are liable on any assets yielding income. The rate is 2.2% on net wealth exceeding 1,083,000 kr.

(v)   **National Welfare Contribution**
Levied on residents at 5.35% on taxable income.

(b) Companies etc.
Company Income Tax *(Indkomstskat af aktieselskaber m.v.):* Charged on net taxable profits (Law for the Taxation of Companies No. 255 of 11th June 1960).

2   INDIVIDUALS' TAXATION

(a) Income charged
Residents (i.e. those domiciled in Denmark or resident over 6 months in the year and, in some cases, former residents and Danish citizens living abroad): Income from all sources
Non-residents: Income derived or received from Denmark.

16

(b) Year and basis of assessment
The normal tax year is the calendar year but a taxpayer may employ another "deviating income year".

(c) Computation of taxable income
Total income, subject to certain exemptions and admissible deductions, is assessed and credit for personal allowances is given against the tax. There is an overall limit to the sum of national income tax, communal and county income taxes, capital tax and national welfare contribution: the total liability is not to exceed 78% of taxable income, and the taxes other than capital tax are not to exceed 70%, national income tax being reduced by the amount of any excess. Married persons are normally jointly assessed, except that a wife's income from independent activities, pensions etc. is separately taxed. Children are assessed separately on their own income. Members of all kinds of partnership are individually liable for tax on their shares of profit.

(i) **Business, professional or agricultural income:**
Basis
Net profits (including certain capital gains) of the tax year, or of the taxpayer's accounting year ending within that year, after admissible deductions and set-off of losses brought forward for up to 5 years.
Depreciation allowances
Allowances for machinery, plant etc. are given on a reducing balance basis, the amount being at the taxpayer's option subject to a maximum of 30% of written down value at the beginning of the year which is adjusted from 1982 for inflation, based on the consumer price index: motor vehicles are depreciated separately, with a restriction on the depreciable amount for each vehicle. Separate provisions apply to ships. Annual allowances for buildings are at specified rates varying in accordance with their purpose.

(ii) **Capital gains**
In general, capital gains on business assets or arising as part of the taxpayer's business are included in the computation of national income tax, as are gains on the sale of shares etc. within 3 years of acquisition. Special income tax (instead of national income tax) may however be charged

in respect of profits from the sale of business goodwill, patent rights etc., lump-sum compensation payments and shares held by a seller with a substantial interest. Profits on sale of real property held less than 7 years are also subject to special income tax, with adjustments dependent on length of ownership.

(iii) Salaries, wages etc., pensions

Income from employment and former employment, including related payments and benefits in kind, is subject to deduction of tax at source at a rate based on expected income. A standard deduction of 5% subject to a maximum of 3,200kr. is allowed for expenses, unless a higher amount can be substantiated. An employee's contributions to certain kinds of superannuation schemes etc. may be deductible in arriving at taxable income. There are special concessions for employees temporarily resident in Denmark.

(iv) Dividends, interest etc.

Dividends and other distributions by companies to non-residents are subject to a final withholding tax at 30%. Interest arising in Denmark is included in taxable income of residents but is exempt in the hands of non-residents. Under the imputation system of corporation tax resident shareholders are entitled to a tax credit of 25%.

(v) Income from letting and leasing

Rents on property received and the rental value of owner-occupied living accommodation, less mortgage interest, repairs and other expenses, are included in taxable income.

(vi) Other income

Miscellaneous taxable income includes betting and gambling winnings and lottery prizes.

(d) Deductions from total income
(i) General deductions

Admissible deductions include (subject to certain conditions and limits) life assurance premiums, loan interest, losses brought forward (for up to 5 years) and charitable donations.

(ii) Personal and other allowances

Personal reliefs include personal allowances for resident

individuals and jointly-taxed spouses, age allowance and an allowance for wife's earned income. Child allowances have been replaced by tax-free child subsidies.

(iii) Tax credits
Amounts available for set-off against the total liability include tax suffered by deduction at source and tax credits attached to dividends under the imputation system.

(e) Tax deducted at source
(i) Employment income: See (c) (iii) above.
(ii) Dividends: See (c) (iv) above.

3 COMPANY INCOME TAX

(a) Types of undertaking charged
Joint-stock companies *(Aktieselskaber)*, including foreign companies. Other associations including co-operative societies and mutual insurance societies.

(b) Income charged
Domestic companies etc. (i.e. those whose head offices or principal administrative establishments are in Denmark): Total net profits
Foreign companies: Net profits derived from property or a business establishment in Denmark.

(c) Computation of taxable income
Net taxable profits are computed under the same general provisions as apply to the business etc. income of individuals. Up to 25% of annual profits may however be allocated free of tax to an investment reserve by companies engaged in trade or business. The tax year for companies ends on March 31st and taxable profits are those of the calendar year or accounting year preceding the tax year. Taxable profits comprise the net income from all the assets of the business, including dividends and interest received and capital gains which, for an individual, would be chargeable to the special income tax (2(c) (ii) above).

4 DOUBLE TAXATION

There are comprehensive double taxation agreements between Denmark and the United Kingdom and also over 40 other countries: in addition, the agreement with the UK has been extended to 26 former British colonial territories and to the Faroe Islands. Unilateral relief is given for tax paid abroad on income arising in a country with which there is no double taxation agreement.

5 RATES OF TAX

The rates of tax are subject to change from year to year, but the sample rates shown below for 1984 (individuals) or 1982/83 (companies) give an indication of recent rates. Amounts are stated in Danish Kroner (kr.). There are provisions to ensure that the overall tax burden of individuals does not exceed a certain percentage of taxable income (see 2(c) above).

(a) *Individuals*

(i) National income tax:

Graduated rates on successive slices of taxable income are subject to adjustment by reference to the wages index, but the actual tax payable is at 90% of the basic rates. The net rates payable range from 14.4% on the first 108,200kr. to 28.8% on the next 70,800kr. and 39.6% on the balance over 179,000kr.

Personal reliefs for residents include:
individual	22,200kr.	given in terms of
jointly-taxed spouses	44,400kr.	tax at 14.4%

(ii) Special income tax:

The charge is at 50% of net special income.

(b) *Companies etc.*

Standard rate of company income tax is 40%.

(c) *Withholding taxes*

Payments to non-resident companies:

	General rate	Rate applied under UK double taxation agreement
Dividends	30%	NIL or 15%*
Interest	NIL	NIL
Royalties	NIL	NIL

* Nil rate for companies owning 25% or more of voting power: on holdings below 25%, the tax credit of 25% less 15% Danish tax is also paid.

FINLAND

Finland has a population of under 5 million in an area larger than that of the United Kingdom, much of the country being occupied by lakes and forests. The two official languages are Finnish and Swedish. The country has close connections with the other Scandinavian countries and also has trade links with the USSR.

Taxes on income comprise a State income tax, with separate final withholding taxes on income paid to non-residents, and local communal and church taxes which are levied at varying rates and are a substantial element in the total weight of taxes. There is also a wealth tax payable by individuals and partnerships and by non-resident companies with a permanent establishment in Finland.

The combined effect of the State and local taxes is to produce a fairly steeply progressive scale of personal taxation, but the top rates are only reached at a high level of income. There is however a ceiling of 80% of taxable income for the total of national and local taxes, including social security and wealth taxes. In general, short-term capital gains are included in ordinary taxable income, but some relatively long-term gains are exempted.

A number of tax incentives are provided for businesses set up in development (or "support") areas, such as free depreciation, tax-free investment reserves and investment allowances. Businesses are permitted to make transfers of profits to special investment reserves which are free of tax provided the funds are eventually used for the purchase of business assets. Agriculture, forestry and ship-building are important in Finland and have special treatment for tax purposes.

Finland

1 LIST OF TAXES

(a) State taxes

(i) State income tax *(Statliginkomstskatt):* levied on the income of individuals and companies etc.

(ii) Withholding tax *(Källskatt):* levied on certain income of non-residents.

(iii) Wealth tax *(Förmögenhetsskatt):* levied on the net wealth of individuals and partnerships on a progressive scale rising, for residents, to 1.7% on the excess over 1,016,000FMk. Married persons are jointly assessed, after a deduction from net wealth of 13,500FMk. plus 6,800FMk. for each child under 16. Non-resident individuals and companies (with a permanent establishment in Finland) are subject to the tax at 1% on assets in Finland other than investments etc. the income on which is subject to the final withholding tax and unless exempted under tax treaties. (Not further dealt with in this summary).

(b) Local taxes (Not further dealt with in this summary)

These taxes are not deductible in computing profits for State income tax purposes.

(i) Communal tax *(Kommunalskatt):* levied on the income of individuals and companies etc. at rates varying between 14% and 18.5% fixed by the communes (e.g. Helsinki 15%): methods of assessment are similar to those for State income tax, but vary in some respects.

(ii) Church tax *(Kyrkoskatt):* levied by parishes at a rate of 1 – 2% on the income of individuals and companies as determined for communal tax.

2 INDIVIDUALS' TAXATION

(a) Income charged

Residents: Income from all sources
Non-residents: Income derived from Finland (largely covered by final withholding taxes).

(b) Year and basis of assessment

The tax year is the calendar year. Tax is assessed on the

income of the preceding year or, in the case of a business, on the income of its accounting period ending in that year. There is a system of monthly advance payments of tax, the amounts paid being adjustable on the basis of the final assessment.

(c) *Computation of taxable income*
Total income, subject to exemptions, less admissible deductions and reliefs, is assessable to income tax. In general, all expenses incurred in acquiring the income are deductible. Married persons are, in principle, assessed separately, but any unearned income, after the first 3,000FMk., of the spouse with the lower (or no) earned income is added to the income of the other spouse for assessment. Partnerships are taxed as separate entities and the members are not individually liable except for salaries from the partnership: the salaries are deducted in computing partnership net profits.

(i) **Business or professional income:**
Basis
Taxable profits are those from all of the assets of the business etc., including taxable capital gains (see (ii) below). Profits are determined on normal commercial principles and no allowances, e.g. for depreciation, are admissible unless they are incorporated in the financial statements. Local taxes paid are not admissible deductions. Allocations of up to 50% of profits may be made to investment reserves, and the amounts transferred are tax free provided the reserves are eventually used for the purchase of business assets: within limits, certain other tax-free allocations to reserves are also permissible. Investment allowances are given for qualifying investments in certain development areas. Losses may be carried forward for up to 5 years.
Depreciation allowances
Depreciation at approved rates on reducing balance methods is allowed on buildings (up to 10%), plant and machinery (up to 30%). Free depreciation and other tax and investment incentives are provided to promote development in "support" areas.

(ii) **Capital gains**
Capital gains on disposal of real property held for over 10

years (or a dwelling house occupied by the taxpayer for over 1 year) and of securities or other assets held for over 5 years are exempt, but shorter term gains are included in taxable income: however, for real property held over 5 years, 20% of the gain is tax-free for each year over 5.

(iii) Special trades
Some special provisions apply to the taxation of profits from agriculture, forestry and ship-building carried on in Finland and the depreciation allowances are different.

(iv) Salaries, wages etc., pensions
Income from employment and former employment, including benefits in kind, is included in taxable income, subject to exemption for some kinds of retirement benefit: a fixed deduction for expenses of 350FMk. plus 4% of salary income (maximum total 1,200FMk.) is allowed unless more can be substantiated and there is a further allowance of 1% (maximum 800FMk.). Tax is deducted at source, based on official tables, credit for the tax deducted being given on the assessment made in the following year. Final withholding tax at 35% is deducted from payments to non-residents.

(v) Dividends, interest etc.
The first 2,750FMk. of dividends received by residents from Finnish companies is exempt. Dividends received by resident individuals are subject to a withholding tax on account of their final liability for State and local taxes. A final withholding tax is deducted from payments to non-residents of dividends (at 25%) and interest (at 30%) in satisfaction of all national and local taxes.

(vi) Income from letting and leasing
Rents received and the rental value of owner-occupied living accommodation, after deduction of an allowance for maintenance etc. expenses, or of buildings used for a business or agriculture, are taxable income.

(vii) Other income
Subject to the provisions of double taxation agreements, final withholding tax at 30% is deducted from royalties (and other kinds of income not specifically provided for) paid to non-residents.

(d) *Deductions from total income*

(i) **General deductions**
In general, allowable deductions include expenses incurred in the acquisition of income, losses and interest paid. Residents may also make limited deductions for life insurance, superannuation contributions and medical expenses.

(ii) **Personal and other allowances**
Residents are eligible for reliefs in respect of earned income, dependent spouse, children and age.

(iii) **Tax credits**
Credit is given against the final assessment for tax suffered by deduction at source from the income of the preceding year on which the assessment is based.

(e) *Tax deducted at source*
(i) Employment income: See (c) (iv) above.
(ii) Dividends, interest etc.: See (c) (v) above.
(iii) Royalties etc.: See (c) (vii) above.

3 COMPANIES' TAXATION

(a) *Types of undertaking charged*
Joint stock companies *(Aktiebolag)*
Cooperative societies
(Limited and ordinary partnerships are taxed as separate entities at the rates applicable to individuals)

(b) *Income charged*
Resident companies (i.e. those which are registered in Finland or have their centre of management there): Income from all sources
Non-resident companies ("foreign companies"): Income derived from Finland.

(c) *Computation of taxable income*
The computation of taxable income is in general in accordance with the same rules as for the business profits of individuals. Capital gains are deal with as in 2 (c)(ii) above and capital losses on business assets are treated as normal business losses. Dividends received by one company from

another are normally exempt from State income tax. For the purpose of computing State income tax, 60% of the excess of dividends paid over exempt dividends received is deductible. In addition, as a temporary measure, the whole of dividends on new share issues of resident companies are treated as deductible. Special tax reliefs are granted to shipbuilding companies, metal or timber industries and public utilities.

4 DOUBLE TAXATION

Double taxation agreements are in force between Finland and the United Kingdom and also over 30 other countries. In addition, unilateral relief is given, whereby tax paid abroad on income arising abroad is deductible from Finnish tax payable on that income for the same period.

5 RATES OF TAX

Rates of tax are subject to change from year to year, but the sample figures shown below for 1983 give an indication of recent rates. Amounts are stated in the Finnish markka (FMk.).

(a) Individuals

Rates of State income tax for residents rise on a graduated scale on successive slices of taxable income, after exemption for the first 12,500FMk., from 6% on the next 4,500FMk. to 28% on 32,000-42,000FMk. and 51% on the excess over 373,000FMk. Non-residents are charged at a fixed 35% on employment income and 30% on other income not covered by final withholding taxes.

Personal reliefs for residents are as follows:

	Deduction from:	
	Taxable income	*State income tax*
Dependent spouse	4,500FMk. (less 25% of any income of dependant)	–
Dependent children	1,400FMk. each	+ 750–1,350FMk. (each under 16)
Age (over 65)	–	100FMk.
Earned income	25% (maximum 9,800FMk.)*	–

*The allowance is increased for dependent children.

If the total of national and local taxes, including social security and wealth tax, exceeds 80% of taxable income, a reduction is allowed.

(b) *Companies*
The standard rate of tax on taxable profit is 43% (plus local income tax as for individuals).

(c) *Withholding taxes*
Payments to non-resident companies:

	General rate	*Rate applied under UK double taxation agreement*
Dividends	25%	5%
Interest	30%	NIL
Royalties	30%	NIL

FRANCE

The French General Tax Code applies throughout the French Union but in the overseas departments there are modifications from the regulations which obtain in metropolitan France. In addition to the national income tax and company tax, there are a number of local taxes, based on notional income calculated in various ways, charges for which are deductible in computing income for the national taxes.

Following the election of the Socialist President Mitterrand in May 1981, a programme of financial stringency was introduced, including amongst other measures a surtax (called a "solidarity tax") on the higher levels of income tax, a surtax on total income and a wealth tax. A number of measures of nationalisation and social reform are also involved.

In general, the principle of "territoriality" is applied, so that profits of a foreign branch or of a transaction wholly completed abroad are not subject to French tax.

The total taxable income of individuals is computed under a number of separate categories of income. Under these categories, various kinds of capital gain are included in taxable income, with different treatment in some headings of short and long-term gains, but the taxability of an individual's gains on disposal of investments depends more on the size and frequency of the gains.

The graduated rates of tax for an individual rise on a fairly steep progressive scale for a single person, but the "family part" system of giving allowances for family responsibilities results in a considerably less steep progression for families. There are provisions for the assessment of an additional tax if a person's "external evidence of wealth" indicates a disposable income higher than that returned for tax purposes: there is for this calculation an official scale of income values to be attributed to such possessions as residences and cars and the number of domestic servants employed.

There are tax exemptions for new businesses in their early years and a number of tax incentives in the form of accelerated depreciation and in other ways, benefiting for instance exporters and businesses in development areas.

There is a comprehensive system of withholding taxes, modified in many cases for non-residents by double taxation agreements which are in force between France and a large number of other countries, including many former dependent territories. The standard rate of company tax is at the relatively high level of 50%.

Monaco is a small independent principality on the Mediterranean coast of France, with which there are close links. Brief mention is made where relevant of the main features of taxation in Monaco.

France

1 LIST OF TAXES AND LEGISLATION

The basic law regulating taxes on income is the General Tax Code *(Le code général des impôts)*, a revised edition of which is published annually. The Code applies to metropolitan France (the European mainland departments and Corsica) and, with modifications, to the overseas departments of Martinique, Guadeloupe, Réunion and Guyane, making up the French Union.

(a) National taxes on income
  (i) Personal income tax *(Impôt sur le revenu):* levied on the income of individuals.
  (ii) Company tax *(Impôt sur les sociétés):* levied on the profits of companies and other associations.

(b) Local taxes (not further dealt with in this summary)
Taxes for the purposes of the departments and communes include:
    Land tax, on owners of land and buildings
    Personal tax, on occupiers of residential property
    Tax on business and professions.
Where based on income these taxes are based on notional, rather than actual, income. The charges are deductible in computing income for income tax purposes, if the relevant income, e.g. the income from the land or buildings, is subject to income tax.

(c) Wealth tax (not further dealt with in this summary)
A wealth tax, first introduced in 1982, is charged on property other than business assets, applying to all such property of resident individuals and French property of non-residents. After exemption of the first 3.4 million F, the rates of tax rise from 0.5% to 1.5% on taxable wealth over 11.2 million F. For 1984, there is a surcharge of 8% of net wealth tax due. Companies are not subject to this tax.

The taxation system of Monaco is briefly mentioned where appropriate.

2 INDIVIDUALS' INCOME TAX

(a) Income charged
Residents: Income from all sources

Non-residents: Income derived from France.
In general, non-residents are treated for computation of tax as married taxpayers without children and are charged at a minimum rate of 25%, unless French tax on total world income would be less. There are exceptions to this rule:

(i) In the case of a person resident in a country with which France has no double taxation agreement, who owns a residence in France: such a person may be assessed on a notional basis of three times the rental value of the residence(s), unless his actual French income is less than that calculated on the notional basis.

(ii) Salaries etc. from French sources – see (c) (iv) below.

(b) Year and basis of assessment
The tax year is the calendar year or, in the case of a business, its accounting period ending therein or attributed thereto. Advance payments of tax may be required, based on two thirds of the tax of the previous year, in two instalments on February 15th and May 15th after the end of the tax year.

(c) Computation of taxable income
Tax is computed separately under the following categories:

Income from land and buildings	See (ii) and (vi)
Industrial and commercial profits	See (i) and (ii)
Remuneration of certain directors and partners	See (iv)
Agricultural profits	See (ii) and (iii)
Salaries, wages etc., pensions and life annuities	See (iv)
Profits from non-commercial occupations	See (i), (ii) and (vii)
Income from movable capital	See (ii) and (v)

From the aggregate of income under the various categories there are general deductions (see (d) below), and a deficit under any category may be set off against other income: a net overall deficit may be carried forward for 5 years. There is also a procedure for computing an assumed income, based on external evidence of wealth, judged on certain criteria such as rental value of residence(s), number of domestic servants and motor cars: if this assumed income is over 75,000F and exceeds that disclosed in the income tax return, an additional special tax at 2% of the assumed income may be charged.

Married persons are normally jointly assessed on the income of the family including dependent children. Members of those partnerships which are not treated as "companies" (see 3.(a) below) are liable for personal income tax on their shares of the partnership income.

In Monaco, apart from the business income tax, for which individuals as well as companies are liable (see 3(c) below), there is no individual income tax. French nationals residing in Monaco remain liable to French income tax.

(i) Business or professional income
Basis

Business profits in the year (or for an accounting period ending in the year) are taxable as "industrial and commercial profits": profits in the year from professional activities are included in the category of "profits from non-commercial occupations". Net profits, after admissible expenses, from all the assets of a business (even though they would otherwise come in another category of income) are treated as industrial and commercial profits: profits from professional activities are total receipts less necessary expenses.

For small businesses and taxpayers with receipts from non-commercial occupations (including professions) under 175,000F in the year, there are arrangements for computing notional assumed profits, based on turnover and other indications, rather than actual profits.

Amounts within specified limits allocated to reserves for certain defined special purposes (e.g. to meet probable losses on debts, raw materials and investments or set aside by mining enterprises for research and exploration) are excluded from the taxable profits of a business until no longer required for the original purposes. Investments in assets abroad may, under certain conditions, be charged to a tax-deductible reserve. A special tax credit is given to smaller concerns which incur increased research expenditure.

Capital gains on realisation of fixed assets of a business or profession are taxable: short-term gains less

losses of the year (i.e. those on assets held for less than 2
years, or for a longer period to the extent that they are
attributable to depreciation allowed for tax purposes)
are taxed as ordinary profit but may be spread over 3
years: long-term gains less losses may be set against
trading losses, but any excess of gain is taxed at 15%.
Capital gains of businesses on disposal of building land
are taxed at 25%: the gains may be offset by ordinary
business losses but not by capital losses on other fixed
assets.

Capital gains on sale of assets by an agricultural
undertaking which is taxed on a notional basis (see (iii)
below) are exempt.

A new tax incentive, introduced in the 1984 Budget,
exempts new industrial enterprises created in 1983 or
1984 from all tax in their first 3 years and 50% for the
next 2 years. The exemption applies both to individuals
and companies.

Depreciation allowances
Amounts written off for depreciation of fixed assets, in
accordance with generally accepted practices for a particular industry, are admissible deductions from profits:
depreciation of private cars is limited to that on a
maximum of 35,000F per car: accelerated depreciation is
allowed in a number of special cases (e.g. assets for
research, or belonging to exporters or in under-developed
areas). Provisions similar to those for businesses etc.
apply to depreciation of assets used for a profession etc.
Extra depreciation allowances are given on additions in
the years 1983-1985 of assets which are subject to
declining balance depreciation (i.e. most assets other
than buildings and short-life assets) at rates varying in
accordance with the life of the assets.

(ii) **Capital gains**
Business, professional or agricultural assets: see (i) above.
Land and buildings: subject to a number of conditions
and exemptions (e.g. for gain on sale of a principal
residence) a part of the capital gains realised by individuals on disposal of building land is included in taxable

income from land and buildings. There is also a special tax (at rates varying between 15% and 33⅓% according to when the building permit was issued) on capital gains on disposal of buildings erected by the vendors. Non-residents are subject to a withholding tax at 33⅓% on such gains.

Shares in companies: capital gains on disposals are taxable (as income from movable capital) under the following circumstances from 1 January 1979:

1. Net gains from "habitual transactions", as defined, carried on by a resident are taxable as ordinary income if they exceed the taxpayer's other income and in other cases either at 30% or as ordinary income, at the taxpayer's option.

2. Net gains from "substantial disposals", as defined (i.e. exceeding 168,000F in a year), made by a resident are taxable at 15%, unless they are treated as coming under 1. above.

3. Capital gains of shareholders (both resident and non-resident) on disposal of shares in a company in which they are entitled to 25% or more of the profits, are taxable at 15%.

(iii) Special trades

Special provisions apply, *inter alia,* to agriculture (which is generally taxed on a notional basis), shipping and air transport, banks, oil and natural gas and construction profits.

(iv) Salaries, wages etc., pensions

Income from employment and former employment, including benefits in kind, is taxable subject to certain exemptions (e.g. war pensions and some compensation payments). In arriving at taxable income, deductions are allowed for superannuation and social insurance contributions and necessary expenses (10% of income or actual expenses if greater, with a minimum of 1,800F and a maximum of 50,900F, but with supplementary deductions for certain occupations). 80% of the first 460,000F of net income after deductions of contributions and expenses, and the whole of the remainder, is included in total income, except that there is a further deduction of 10%, with a maximum of 21,400F, from pensions and retirement benefits. Lump-sum payments on retirement not exceeding 10,000F are exempt.

Tax is deductible at source from payments of income in this category to non-residents from French sources, at 15% of annual amounts between 40,900F and 118,900F and 25% of larger amounts: for French nationals the deduction is a final withholding tax.

The remuneration of certain directors and partners (i.e. majority shareholders and managing partners) is in a separate category of income, tax being based on total income less relevant expenses.

There are provisions for compulsory sharing of profits with their employees by businesses with more than 100 employees.

(v) Dividends, interest etc.
Dividends and interest are taxable as "income from movable capital".

In respect of dividends and other distributions of profits made by French companies and other associations liable to company tax:

1. Resident shareholders (other than parent companies) are entitled to a tax credit *(avoir fiscal)* of 50% of the dividend, which is set off against their tax liability.

2. Non-resident shareholders: a final withholding tax at 25% (subject to the provisions of double taxation agreements) is deducted.

The first 3,000F of dividend income of individuals whose taxable income does not exceed a certain amount (currently 280,000F) is however exempt from tax.

Interest payments are treated as follows:

1. Bonds and loans represented by negotiable securities: a withholding tax at 10% is deductible from payments of interest, increased to a compulsory deduction *(prélèvement obligatoire)* of 25%, subject to the provisions of

double taxation agreements, from payments to non-residents.

2. Unsecured loans, deposit interest etc.: subject to certain exemptions, tax at 38% or 45% is deductible at source from interest payments.

Resident individual recipients of interest of either of the above types may elect to have a deduction made at 38% (or for some types of interest 25% or 33⅓%) *(prélèvement liberatoire):* such deductions represent the recipient's final tax liability on the income in question. The first 5,000F of most kinds of bond interest is however exempt from tax. Dividends and interest received by residents from foreign sources are subject to French tax.

(vi) Income from letting and leasing

Income from land and buildings, other than income from buildings etc. let for agricultural purposes or owner-occupied, is taxable: admissible deductions include losses from previous years, repairs and maintenance, interest and a standard allowance of 15% of gross income on urban properties for administration and depreciation, or 10% for rural properties.

(vii) Other income

The income category of "profits from non-commercial occupations" covers sources of profit and income which do not fall within other categories (e.g. certain royalties and fees). A withholding tax at 33⅓% is deductible from payments of fees and royalties to individuals and companies with no fixed base in France, subject to the provisions of double taxation agreements.

(d) Deductions from total income

(i) General deductions

Admissible deductions include life insurance premiums (within limits), deficits of the year in any income category and unrecovered losses of the previous 5 years brought forward.

Subject to certain limits and conditions, taxpayers are entitled to a deduction from total net income of the amount of their new investment (purchases less sales) in the year in certain kinds of French securities, including shares officially quoted and some others.

(ii) **Personal and other allowances**
Relief is given to taxpayers in recognition of their marital status and number of dependants by a "family part" *(quotient familial)* system, on the general basis of one "part" for a single person, with an additional "part" for a married couple and an additional half "part" for each dependent child (other than the second child for which a whole additional "part" is allowed). The income limit for each step on the graduated tax scale is multiplied by the number of "parts" applicable to the taxpayer, so that the amount of income on which tax is payable at the lower rates is increased according to his family responsibilities.

(iii) **Tax credits**
Tax suffered by deduction at source (except where it is specified to be a final withholding tax – e.g. the *"prélèvement liberatoire"* referred to at (c) (v) above) and credits under double taxation agreements are available for credit against the final liability of a taxpayer.

(e) Tax deducted at source
(i) Capital gains	See (c) (ii) above.
(ii) Employment income	See (c) (iv) above.
(iii)Dividends, interest etc.	See (c) (v) above.
(iv) Fees, royalties etc.	See (c) (vii) above.

3 COMPANY TAX

(a) Types of undertaking charged
The following types of association *(société)* are liable to company tax and are referred to under the general description of "companies":

Public limited companies *(sociétés anonymes – abbreviation SA)*
Private limited companies *(sociétés à responsabilité limitée – abbreviation SARL)*
Limited partnerships with share capital
Other kinds of partnership which have so elected (the election is irrevocable)

Co-operative societies and other associations which carry
on business activities
Foreign companies

(b) *Income charged*
French and foreign companies are both liable for company
tax on profits from undertakings carried on in France. French
companies may elect for the tax to be based on world income,
subject to agreement of the authorities: credit for overseas
tax is given, up to the rate of French company tax, and any
excess is allowed as a credit carried forward.

A non-resident foreign company with property at its
disposal in France is liable for company tax on three times
the rental value of the property, payable by the occupier.

(c) *Computation of taxable income*
The computation of taxable income is in general in accordance with the same rules as for the industrial and commercial
profits of individuals, so far as applicable, and is based on
actual income (the notional basis referred to at 2.(c) (i) not
being applicable). Companies which pay dividends out of
profits on which company tax at 50% has not been paid are
charged a prepayment *(précompte)* at 50%, equivalent to
the tax credit *(avoir fiscal)* on the dividend. Inter-company
dividends where there is a holding of 10% or more are 95%
exempted. Companies formed, or increasing their capital, in
the years 1983-1987 may, in general, deduct dividends distributed on the new capital in computing taxable profits for the
first 10 years.

Capital gains are taxable as for individuals, but the
balance of any long-term gains after tax is put into a special
reserve and any appropriation from this is included in
ordinary taxable profits.

Enterprises with over 100 employees are required to
contribute to special reserves for profit-sharing. The contribution is deductible from taxable income of the following
year. Certain tax-free reserves for acquisition of fixed assets
may also be set up.

Tax is payable automatically without notice of assessment. Quarterly advance payments are required based on
9/10ths of the previous year's profits.

In Monaco, companies operating in the principality are

exempt from the business income tax unless at least 25% of their turnover arises from operation outside Monaco. As an incentive to the establishment in Monaco of headquarters of foreign companies, such offices are chargeable to business income tax only on 8% of their running expenses.

4 DOUBLE TAXATION

Comprehensive double taxation agreements are in force between France and the United Kingdom and also over 50 other countries. The tax credit attaching to a dividend from a United Kingdom company may be claimed by a resident of France (other than by a company controlling 10% or more of the UK company): UK tax at 15% is then chargeable on the dividend plus tax credit and French tax may also be charged on the total, credit being given for the UK tax.

5 RATES OF TAX

The rates of tax are subject to variation from year to year but the figures shown below for 1983 income give an indication of recent rates in metropolitan France. Amounts are stated in French francs (F).

(a) Individuals

There is a graduated scale of income tax per "family part" (see 2.(d) (ii) above) on successive slices of net taxable income, rising from nil on the first 13,770F per family part to 5% on 13,771–14,390F, 25% on 34,701–43,610F, and 65% on the excess over 212,750F per family part: no income tax is chargeable where an individual's income net of employment expenses does not exceed 27,000F (29,500F for individuals over 65 years of age). Persons over 65 and invalids etc. are allowed a deduction of 5,920F if their taxable income does not exceed 36,600F or 2,960F on taxable income up to 59,200F.

There is a 1% surtax on 1983 income, including income from capital gains and that subject to final withholding taxes. This surtax was first introduced by an "austerity package" law of 25 March 1983 and the revenue from it goes to a social security equalisation fund.

France

There is, in addition, a surcharge on total income tax which, for tax on 1983 income, is 5% on tax between 20,001F and 30,000F and 8% thereafter.

The tax relief for dependent children (see 2(d) (ii) above) is limited to 9,250F per half part.

(b) Companies

The standard rate of company tax is 50% and the minimum tax payable per annum is 3,000F: for companies with turnover of over 1 million F, by a change made in the 1984 Budget, this minimum rises in stages to 15,000F where turnover exceeds 10 million F.

(c) Withholding taxes

Payments to non-resident companies:

	General rate	Rate applied under UK double taxation agreement
Dividends	25%	5% or 15%*
Interest	25%**	10% or 12%***
Royalties	33⅓%	NIL

* The lower rate to a company owning 10% or more of voting power. A UK resident company with less than 10% of voting power is entitled to receive also the tax credit *(avoir fiscal)* of 50% of the dividend less French tax at 15%.

** Or higher rates on some kinds of interest.

*** The higher rate on bonds issued before 1 January 1965.

(d) Monaco

The rate of business income tax is 35%.
There are no withholding taxes.

GERMANY

The Federal Republic of Germany, which includes West Berlin, is a prosperous democracy. There are no restrictions on foreign investment in the country, but at the same time there are no special tax incentives designed to attract the registration of foreign businesses. A high proportion of industrial finance is provided by long-term borrowing, mainly from banks, rather than in the form of equity capital.

In addition to income tax or corporation tax, a substantial further burden of direct taxation arises from the federal capital tax on wealth and the business tax levied by the communes, though the business tax is a deductible expense for income or corporation tax purposes.

Personal rates of income tax are on a progressive scale but the rate on the top range of income is not particularly high and the "income-splitting" methods used effectively make the progression less steep for families. There is a modest form of wealth tax ("Capital Tax") payable by resident individuals and companies on total capital and by non-residents on capital situated within the Federal Republic. Capital gains tax is charged on the disposal of a business, and gains realised by a business are normally taxed as ordinary income: there are also provisions for taxing short-term gains from "speculative" transactions in non-business assets.

Companies pay corporation tax at a higher rate on undistributed profits than on distributions. Tax incentives provided, in the form of accelerated depreciation allowances and tax rebates, are mainly for development regions (and in particular, West Berlin) where additional employment is wanted. A tax imputation system is in force. There are double taxation agreements with a large number of countries.

Germany

(The Federal Republic of Germany, including West Berlin)

1 LIST OF TAXES

(a) Taxes on income
  (i) Income Tax *(Einkommensteuer):* discharged in part by deductions at source in respect of:
  Wages tax *(Lohnsteuer)*
  Capital yields tax *(Kapitalertragsteuer)*
  Directors tax *(Aufsichtsratsteuer)*
  A tax imputation system is in force.
  (ii) Corporation Tax *(Körperschaftsteuer)*

(b) Other taxes (not further referred to in this summary)
  (i) Capital Tax *(Vermögensteuer):* a form of wealth tax payable by resident individuals and companies on total capital and by non-resident aliens on capital situated within the Federal Republic. Normal rates are 0.5% for individuals and 0.6% for companies, with exemptions for the initial slice of capital of individuals and for certain business assets. Tax paid is not deductible for income or corporation tax purposes.
  (ii) Business Tax *(Gewerbesteuer):* a local tax on profits and capital of business enterprises at varying rates fixed by the communes (usually 15% on income and 0.6% on capital): tax paid is deductible in arriving at federal income for taxation purposes.

2 LEGISLATION

The Income Tax Law of 5 December 1977 and the Corporation Tax Law of 31 August 1976 are implemented and given detailed effect by regulations published by decree.

3 INCOME TAX – INDIVIDUALS

(a) Income charged
  Residents   Total income from all sources
  Non-residents Income arising in the Federal Republic (with extensions in certain circumstances for German nationals)

(b) **Year and basis of assessment**
Industrial, commercial and professional undertakings: accounting year ending in the tax year
Other individuals: tax year
Agricultural etc. activities: year ended 30th June
The tax year is the calendar year.

(c) **Computation of taxable income**
Tax is calculated under the following separate categories, from the aggregate of which there are personal and other reliefs. Married persons are jointly assessed unless they elect separate assessments: when jointly assessed, tax is computed (for residents only) on an "income-splitting" method at twice the amount of tax due on half the joint income. Members of ordinary partnerships are individually liable for tax on their shares of income.

(i) **Industrial and commercial profits:**
Basis
Taxable profits are normally based on changes in the value of net assets in the balance sheets for successive accounting years, after adjusting for additions and disposals: if proper accounting records are not maintained, assessments may be based on estimates.

The value of assets is generally taken at cost less depreciation but a "part-valuation" *(Teilwert)* on a going-concern basis may be substituted.

Losses exceeding 5 million DM, not recovered from other income of the year, may be carried forward for up to 5 years.

Depreciation allowances
Movable assets: straight-line or reducing balance methods, maximum rates being specified: for assets on the "part-valuation" basis (see above), the straight-line method is used: small amounts may be written off in full.

Buildings and intangible assets: straight-line basis: special provisions apply e.g. for double-shift working or for industries in West Berlin.

Aircraft, ships, R & D assets: these and some other special categories are eligible for special allowances.

Mines, quarries etc.: depletion allowances.

(ii) Capital gains:
Disposal of business or part business
Gains over a specified minimum amount are liable to tax as extraordinary income at half the normal rate.
Sale of business assets
Gains realised by a business enterprise are normally taxable as ordinary income: under certain conditions, "roll-over" relief is applied and a gain is not taxed but deducted from acquisition costs of replacement asset for depreciation purposes.
Speculative transactions
Short-term gains exceeding 1,000DM on real estate held less than 2 years and on other non-business assets held less than 6 months are taxable as ordinary income.
Substantial holdings in companies
Gains over 20,000DM on sales of holdings of 25% or more are taxable at half the normal rate.

(iii) Agricultural and professional activities
Computation of profits and capital gains is subject to some special provisions, but in the main is on the same lines as for industrial undertakings. Fees of artists, journalists etc. from independent personal services in Germany are subject to withholding tax at 15%.

(iv) Salaries, wages etc., pensions
Remuneration from employment and former employment is taxable subject to certain exemptions (e.g. reimbursed expenses) and deductions (e.g. allowance for costs incurred): tax is deducted at source (wages tax).

(v) Dividends, interest etc.
Liable income from movable capital includes dividends (and other distributions of profit) and interest, subject to certain exemptions: special provisions are made for bonus share issues and employees' profit sharing or share purchase schemes: tax is deducted at source (capital yields tax). The 36% tax on distributions of German companies is imputed against resident individual and corporate shareholders' liabilities and credit is also given for the 25% tax withheld at source.

(vi) **Income from letting and leasing**

Income from property (including "utility value" of tax-payer's residence), leasing of business assets, building and mineral rights, copyrights and patent royalties is assessed under this heading. Royalties are subject to the deduction of withholding tax.

(vii) **Other income**

Short-term capital gains, annuity income and casual profits subject to certain deductions and exemptions are included in taxable income.

(d) *Deductions from total income*

(i) **General deductions**

Standard allowances are granted (increased within limits if higher expenditure substantiated) for certain special expenses including e.g. annuities payable, charitable and political donations, life insurance, Social Security contributions: partial exemption is given for employers' contributions for compulsory insurance cover and voluntary health insurance.

The allowances as above for "special expenses" are additional to income-related expenses deductible in arriving at net taxable income from employment, investments and annuities, for which there are standard amounts unless higher amounts can be justified.

(ii) **Personal allowances**

Fixed allowances are given, increased for a single tax-payer caring for a child (see 6 (a) below). Child allowances, in addition to tax-free child subsidies, have been re-introduced from 1983.

(iii) **Age relief**

Fixed allowances are given according to age, increased for any pensions of taxpayers over 65 years of age.

(iv) **Non-residents**

A special fixed allowance is given but tax on German-source income must be at a minimum rate of 25%.

(v) **West Berlin income**

Special tax rebates are given.

(vi) Reduced rates of tax
Taxable capital gains, income from scientific, artistic etc. work and from agriculture etc. and some other special receipts may be taxed at half the average applicable rate.

(e) Tax deducted at source

(i) Independent personal services
See (c) (iii) above.

(ii) Wages tax
See (c) (iv) above: credit is given for wages tax deductions in tax assessment on total income.

(iii) Capital yields tax
See (c) (v) above: credit is given to residents for capital yields tax deductions in tax assessments on total income: the tax liability of non-residents is discharged by the capital yields tax deduction or net dividend paid unless the income is in the category of profits of a business carried on in the Federal Republic.

(iv) Royalties
See (c) (vi) above)

(v) Directors tax
A uniform tax at 30% on fees received by non-resident supervisory directors from domestic companies.

4 CORPORATION TAX – COMPANIES ETC.

(a) Types of undertaking charged
Public limited companies *(Aktiengesellschaften – abbreviation AG)*
Private limited companies *(Gesellschaften mit beschränkter Haftung – abbreviation GmbH)*
Limited partnerships with share capital
Cooperative societies
Mutual assurance companies

(b) Income charged
German resident companies etc.: Net profits from all sources
Foreign companies: Net profits from activities carried on in the Federal Republic and other income taxed by withholding at source.

(c) Computation of taxable income

(i) Basis

Computations are in the main as for income tax on industrial etc. profits of an individual (see 3 (c) (i) above) but subject to certain additional deductible expenses.

(ii) Capital gains

All capital gains of companies are taxed in full as ordinary income.

(iii) Dividends etc. received

The net amount grossed up for corporation tax is included in profits: credit is given against the total tax liability in respect of capital yields tax deducted at source and the corporation tax suffered.

(iv) Relief for foreign tax

German resident companies may, subject to certain conditions, claim relief for foreign tax paid by subsidiaries resident abroad on profits distributed to the parents as dividends.

(v) West Berlin profits

A tax rebate is given in respect of business income arising in West Berlin.

(vi) Investment companies

Special provisions apply.

5 DOUBLE TAXATION AGREEMENTS

General agreements on income and profits are in force between the Federal Republic and the United Kingdom and also about 50 other countries. Unilateral relief may be given for tax suffered in other countries.

6 RATES OF TAX

The rates of tax are subject to change from year to year, but the samples shown below for 1983 give some indication of recent rates.

(a) Individuals

The amounts shown below in DM *(Deutschmark)* are for single persons and for married persons electing separate assessments but, for married persons jointly assessed, personal and age allowances are doubled.

The total net income of a resident taxpayer is reduced, to arrive at taxable income, by deduction of:

Child allowance (each)	432DM
Additional to single parent for caring for child	4,212DM
Age allowance: single persons over 65	720DM
pensions if over 65 40% (max. 4,800DM)	
married persons over 65 (each)	720DM
Earned income and Christmas exemptions	1,080DM
Any "special expenses"	

On taxable income, rates of income tax for individuals on successive slices of income are:

Up to 4,212DM	Nil
4,213DM to 18,000DM	22%
18,001DM upwards	Progressive rates rising to 56% for over 130,019DM

For married couples jointly assessed, the above bases are doubled.

For non-residents, there is a tax-free allowance of 864DM and a minimum rate of tax of 25%. Special tax rebates are given on West Berlin income.

Capital yields tax	25%
Directors tax	30%
Payment to non-residents generally	25%

A law of 20 December 1982 provides for an "Investment Aid Levy" to finance residential building in 1983-1985. 5% of the income tax due (after the first 15,000DM for single and 30,000DM for married persons) is levied as an interest-free loan for at least 3 years. The liability is reduced if certain qualifying investments are made. Non-residents whose income is wholly subject to withholding taxes are not liable for the levy.

(b) Companies etc.

The general rate of corporation tax on undistributed income is 56% (reduced for some types of body such as banks) and on distributed income is 36%.

Non-resident companies with a permanent establishment in Germany pay a flat rate of 50% on income derived therefrom. There are tax rebates for West Berlin companies.

Companies are also liable for a 5% "Investment Aid Levy" on corporation tax, similar to that for individuals referred to above.

(c) *Withholding taxes*
Payments to non-resident companies:

	General rate	Rate applied under UK double taxation agreement
Dividends	25%	15% or 20%*
Interest (certain fixed interest bonds)	25%	NIL
Royalties	25%	NIL

*Higher rate to company owning 25% or more of voting power.

GIBRALTAR

Gibraltar is a very small territory of 2¼ square miles in a peninsula from Southern Spain. It is dependent on, and has very close connections with the United Kingdom, but is largely self-governing. Development is somewhat restricted by the small and densely populated area available. There are however taxation incentives for development projects likely to benefit the local economy: there are also special tax benefits for companies approved as "exempt companies" which are registered in Gibraltar but trade outside the country and are controlled by outside shareholders.

The scale of taxation of individuals shows only a moderate progressive increase for higher incomes, and there is no capital gains tax. There are no double taxation agreements, but unilateral relief is available for income arising in the United Kingdom and other parts of the Commonwealth.

1 LIST OF TAXES AND LEGISLATION

Income tax is levied on the income of individuals and companies under the Income Tax Ordinance (Chapter 76, 1977 Reprint) as amended by subsequent legislation.

2 INDIVIDUALS' TAXATION

(a) Income charged

Residents: Income accruing in, derived from or received in Gibraltar and dividends, interest or emoluments arising outside Gibraltar if they are not taxed in the country of accrual and are received in Gibraltar.

Non-residents: Income accruing in or derived from Gibraltar.

(b) Year and basis of assessment

The year of assessment ends on 30th June. Income from employment etc. is assessed on a current year basis, and other income on the preceding year basis: a business, profession etc. may be assessed on the basis of its accounting year ending in the preceding year.

(c) Computation of taxable income

Aggregate income (subject to certain exemptions), less permissible deductions for losses and for expenses wholly and exclusively incurred in the production of the income, is assessable. Married persons are jointly assessed except, in some cases, where a wife has earned income. Members of partnerships are individually assessed on their shares of income.

(i) Business or professional income:

Basis

The taxable income of the preceding year or accounting period ending in that year. For certain development projects approved for Development Aid, no tax is payable until aggregate net profits exceed the initial capital expenditure.

Depreciation allowances

Wear and tear allowances of reasonable amounts are given in respect of plant, machinery, fixtures and premises used for a business, profession etc. An initial

51

allowance of 100% may be granted, but not for buildings or private cars.

(ii) Capital gains

There is no provision for taxation of capital gains.

(iii) Special trades etc.

Special provisions apply to cable and wireless telegraphy, insurance, shipping and air transport.

(iv) Salaries, wages etc., pensions

Income from employment and former employment, including allowances and benefits: tax is deducted at source under a PAYE system.

(v) Dividends, interest etc.

Tax at 40% is deductible at source from dividends paid by companies ordinarily resident in Gibraltar: tax is normally deductible from interest at the rate applicable to the payee – companies 40%, individuals 30%. Interest on some Government loans and the first £200 of Savings Bank interest are exempt from tax.

(vi) Income from letting and leasing

Rents etc. from property and the net annual value of property other than owner-occupied property are included in taxable income.

(vii) Other income

Miscellaneous taxable income includes royalties and fees for management consultancy etc. services: tax is withheld from such payments to non-residents. Tax may also be withheld from payments to construction sub-contractors.

(d) Deductions from total income

(i) General deductions

Admissible expenses and losses not deducted in arriving at assessable income under sources in (c) above. Unrelieved losses may be carried forward for future recovery.

(ii) Personal and other allowances

Reliefs include personal allowances and allowances for wife, children, dependants and life assurance. Proportionate personal reliefs are allowed to non-resident British subjects (subject to certain restrictions) but not to other non-residents.

(iii) Tax credits
Credit is given for tax suffered by deduction at source and for double taxation relief.

(e) Tax deducted at source
(i) Employment income   See (c) (iv) above.
(ii) Dividends, interest etc.   See (c) (v) above.
(iii) Miscellaneous income   See (c) (vii) above.

3 COMPANIES' TAXATION

(a) Types of undertaking charged
Companies incorporated or registered under the law of Gibraltar or any other country.

(b) Income charged
The chargeable income of resident and non-resident companies is as for individuals (2 (a) above). A company is treated as resident if managed and controlled in Gibraltar or by persons ordinarily resident there.

(c) Computation of taxable income
The computation of tax is in general in accordance with the same rules as for individuals, so far as applicable. Certain companies registered in Gibraltar, dealing in and managing assets outside Gibraltar, may be treated as exempt from income tax (including tax on bank etc. interest earned in Gibraltar) and liable only to a fixed annual tax of £200 or £225.

4 DOUBLE TAXATION

Gibraltar has no double taxation agreements. Relief is allowed for United Kingdom tax charged on income which is also chargeable in Gibraltar. Partial relief is given in respect of income tax chargeable in other countries of the Commonwealth, subject to reciprocal arrangements applying.

5 RATES OF TAX

The effective rates of tax are subject to change from year to year, but the sample rates shown below for the year 1981-82 give an indication of recent rates. Amounts are stated in Gibraltar pounds (£) which are on par with sterling.

(a) Individuals
Standard rate of income tax 30%.
For resident individuals and non-resident British subjects:

Reduced rate first £700 of taxable income (i.e. after personal reliefs)	20%
Additional tax on excess of taxable income over £3,700: first £3,000	5%
next £2,500	10%
next £2,500	15%
balance	20%

Personal reliefs include:

Personal allowance	£850
Wife	£850

Children, wife's earned income, dependent relatives etc.

(b) Companies
Standard rate 40%.

(c) Withholding taxes
Payments to non-resident companies:

	General rate	(No UK double taxation agreement in force)
Dividends	*	
Interest	40%	
Royalties	40%	

*Tax deemed to be deducted at the company rate charged on the profits out of which dividends paid – not a true withholding tax.

GREECE

Greece became a full member of the EEC in 1981. A VAT system required under the terms of the Treaty of Accession has not yet been introduced and the due date has been postponed to 1 January 1986. The country is largely agricultural apart from the main centres of population in Athens and Salonica, but the shipping industry is traditionally very important and tourism has developed on a large scale.

Personal taxation is on a progressive scale, and there are taxes additional to the income tax, raising the effective rate of taxation, the most important of which is a surcharge for Agricultural Social Security. There is no taxation of capital gains except those arising on the disposal of capital assets of a business, which are, with certain exceptions, taxable as ordinary income, and there is no form of wealth tax. Elaborate regulations are in force for assessing notional income based on the evidence of living expenditure etc. where this calculation indicates an income higher than that declared.

There is a full system of tax deductions at source withheld from payments of income to non-residents, and some tax is also collected from residents in this way. Some of the smaller kinds of business concern are not required to maintain complete accounting systems (as are larger businesses) and the method of assessing tax in their case is modified accordingly.

Companies are taxed only on their retained net profits, distributions being taxed in the hands of shareholders.

The Greek authorities have provided a number of incentives, giving tax and other advantages, designed to encourage investment and development, and in particular to promote activity in areas other than the main centres. Some of these incentives are equally available for either domestic or foreign productive investment in the country, while others are specifically aimed at attracting foreign capital.

Greece

1 LIST OF TAXES AND LEGISLATION

Income tax on individuals (Law No. 3323 of 12 August 1955, as amended)
Income tax on companies and other legal entities (Law No. 3843 of 30 September 1958, as amended)

2 INDIVIDUALS' INCOME TAX

(a) *Income charged*

Residents	Income from all sources
Non-residents	Income from Greek sources

(b) *Year and basis of assessment*

The tax year is the calendar year and tax returns are submitted on this basis. An advance payment of tax is required, made in 10 monthly instalments commencing in March. This is based on 50% of the liability on the previous year's income as shown in the return (less tax suffered by deduction at source) together with the balance remaining due on the income of the year before that, after the payments on account made during the previous year.

(c) *Computation of taxable income*

Taxable income is assessed under 7 separate categories, as income from:

1. Buildings
2. Leasing of land
3. Investments
4. Business
5. Farming
6. Employment
7. Professional activities and other sources

The income from these seven sources is aggregated, a loss in one category being set off against other income: from this total, personal allowances, losses from business or farming brought forward from the previous year and some other deductions (see (d) below) may be made. There are exemptions for certain kinds of income, some of which are mentioned under the separate headings which follow.

In order to deal with the understatement of income in tax returns, taxable income may be determined on the basis of the living expenditure of a taxpayer where this is more than 20% higher than the income declared.

Married persons are normally separately assessed. Members of a "limited liability company" *(Etairia Periorismenis Efthynis* or "EPE", with capital contributed in "parts" and not divided into shares, as distinct from a public limited company) and members of a partnership are individually liable for tax on their shares of income.

(i) Business or professional income:

Basis

The net taxable income of a business is computed after deducting reasonable expenditure incurred for the purpose of the business or to produce revenue ("productive" expenditure): capital expenditure is not an admissible deduction. Losses of manufacturing, mining and hotel businesses may be carried forward for 5 years and losses of commercial concerns for 3 years.

Net professional taxable income consists of gross fees etc. less 25% for expenses (up to a maximum of Drs.35,000).

Depreciation allowances

There is no specific provision for including depreciation in the admissible expenditure of the business of an individual, but see 3.(c) below as to companies.

(ii) Capital gains

There is no general taxation of capital gains but realised gains on disposal of capital assets of a business are usually taxable as ordinary income: exemptions are disposals of real property or ships or of plant and machinery whose proceeds are re-invested in the business. There are exceptions to this, including for instance gains on disposal of intangible assets (goodwill, patents etc.) which are taxed at a flat 30%.

(iii) Special trades

Special provisions apply to the taxation of shipping, foreign airline companies and construction activities. Greek shipping companies pay an annual tax based on age, tonnage and category of ships, but their profits, and dividends paid therefrom, are exempt from income tax. Farming is a separate category of income: the first

Drs.200,000 is exempt or the first Drs.500,000 for working farmers.

(iv) Salaries, wages etc., pensions

All kinds of income from employment and former employment, including benefits in kind, are assessable after a deduction of up to 40% of the income, with a maximum deduction of Drs.90,000. Tax on employment income is withheld at source by the employer. Journalists, artists, public entertainers etc. are allowed certain special exemptions. Directors' remuneration and fees are treated as income from movable capital, along with dividends and interest.

(v) Dividends, interest etc.

Certain income from investments is exempt from tax, including:

1. Interest on bank deposits and some kinds of savings account.
2. Interest on national loans.
3. The first Drs.25,000 per annum of dividends from each company listed on the Athens Stock Exchange with a maximum total annual exemption of Drs.100,000.
4. Dividends from Greek shipping companies.

Taxes are deducted at source at the following rates, subject to the effect of double taxation agreements:

1. From dividends: on shares listed on the Athens Stock Exchange, registered 38%, bearer 41%: on unlisted shares, registered 43%, bearer 47%.
   Tax deducted from dividends on bearer shares is a final withholding tax.
2. From interest, at varying rates according to the status of the payer and payee and whether or not they are resident.

(vi) Income from letting and leasing

Income from leasing of land is a separate category of income. The first Drs.48,000 of imputed rental of an owner-occupied house is exempt.

(vii) Other income

Royalties paid by one Greek enterprise to another or to a foreigner with a permanent establishment in Greece are not subject to tax deductions at source: payments to other foreigners are subject to withholding tax at rates varying between 10% and 17.25%. Stamp tax at 2.4% is also deducted from all royalties.

Other miscellaneous types of income from which tax is deducted at source are:

1. Compensation to dismissed employees (if it exceeds Drs.6,000 per month or Drs.250 per day) is paid less a final withholding tax of 10%.
2. Certain professional fees (e.g. to doctors, lawyers or accountants) are paid less 8% income tax plus 1.2% stamp tax (not a final tax).
3. Fees to constructional contractors are paid less 1.5% tax (not a final tax).

(d) Deductions from total income

(i) General deductions

Admissible deductions include medical expenses, life and accident insurance premiums (within prescribed limits), rental payments on a residence (within prescribed limits) and certain kinds of bank interest paid. The previous year's "OGA" surtax (see 5. below) is also deductible.

(ii) Personal and other allowances

Single and married personal allowances and allowances for children and other dependants are given to residents.

(iii) Tax credits

Credit is given for tax suffered by deduction at source, except where this is a final withholding tax; in the latter case, the income in question is not included in the recipient's tax return.

(e) Tax deducted at source

   (i) Employment income   See (c) (iv) above.
   (ii) Dividends, interest etc.   See (c) (v) above.
   (iii)Royalties and miscellaneous income See (c) (vii) above.

3 COMPANIES' ETC. INCOME TAX

(a) Types of undertaking charged
Greek public limited companies (limited by shares, and including "Anonymos Etairia" or "A.E." in their name), but not "limited liability companies" (see 2.(c) above).
Branches of foreign companies.
Other foreign businesses with any form of organisation.
Certain other legal entities (e.g. cooperatives).

(b) Income charged
Resident companies etc.: Income from all sources
Non-resident companies etc.: Income from Greek sources or derived from a permanent establishment in Greece.

(c) Computation of taxable income
Taxable income is normally gross income of the accounting period ending in the preceding year less admissible expenses and dividends distributed. In the main, the computation of taxable income is in accordance with the same rules as for individuals, so far as applicable. The tax year is the company's fiscal year, which must end on either 31 December or 30 June. Business enterprises are required by law to maintain accounting records of degrees of completeness which vary according to the form of organisation and size of turnover. If the authorities reject the taxpayer's accounting records, or if the enterprise is one which is permitted to keep simplified records, tax may be assessed on a percentage of gross income.

Public limited companies are required to provide depreciation on their fixed assets and maximum rates of depreciation acceptable for tax purposes are laid down by law, accelerated rates being permitted in certain cases. Advance payment of tax, amounting to 50% of the previous year's liability, plus tax withheld on distributions, is required in 8 monthly instalments.

Provision has been made for a number of incentives intended to attract foreign investment in businesses of certain types (e.g. manufacturing), or those promoting development outside the Athens–Piraeus area or increasing exports. The main headings under which tax incentives are provided are:
1. Productive investments of foreign capital, for which favourable rates of tax and certain exemptions are granted.

2. Headquarters offices established in Greece, but carrying on business only outside Greece, and bringing in foreign exchange to cover operating expenses, are given exemption from tax on all income earned abroad.
3. Large productive investments, funded by either Greek or foreign capital, are eligible for favourable tax rates and other privileges.
4. Medium and small productive investments in manufacturing enterprises incorporated in Greece may make non-taxable allocations to reserves.
5. Regional development programmes provide for tax reductions etc.
6. Tourist enterprises qualify for tax reductions etc.

4 DOUBLE TAXATION

Comprehensive double taxation agreements are in force between Greece and the United Kingdom and also about 10 other countries. In addition to any other provisions, unilateral relief is given for foreign tax on income from abroad up to the amount of Greek tax on the same income.

5 RATES OF TAX

Rates of tax are subject to change from year to year, but the sample figures shown below for 1983 give an indication of recent rates. Amounts are stated in drachmae (Drs.).

(a) Individuals
Income tax is levied on a progressive scale on successive slices of taxable income, rising, after an initial exemption of Drs.80,000, from 11% on the next Drs.53,000 to 42% on Drs.830,001-1,000,000 and 60% on the excess over Drs.5,300,000. Additional taxes are:

(i) Surtax for agricultural social security (OGA) calculated as a percentage of the income tax liability, 10% on the first Drs.60,000 and 15% of the balance.

(ii) Supplementary tax of 3% on certain income such as interest, directors' fees and profits of a "limited liability company".

(iii) Water supply and drainage tax of 3% on income from buildings in the Athens–Piraeus and Salonica areas.

Personal reliefs deductible by residents in computing taxable income include:

Single allowance	Drs.20,000
Wife	Drs.20,000
Children 1 – 2	Drs.15,000 each
3rd	Drs.25,000
others	Drs.35,000 each
Other dependants	Drs.15,000

There are also additional personal allowances, given as tax credits of Drs.4,800 for a wife and further amounts for children. There is no refund if tax credits exceed the liability.

(b) Companies etc.

Standard rate on retained net profits		Total
less OGA surtax	45%	effective
Agricultural Social Security (OGA)		rate 48.5%
surtax on income tax	15%	approx.

Reduced rates apply to mining or manufacturing profits of a company listed on the Athens Stock Exchange: 35% + OGA surcharge = 38.25%. The 45% rate is applied to all non-resident companies. There are reductions in other cases such as cooperatives.

(c) Withholding taxes

Payments to non-resident companies:

	General rate	*Rate under UK double taxation agreement*
Dividends: Companies listed on the Athens Stock Exchange	42%	42%
Dividends: Other companies (Rates on bearer shares are higher)	47%	47%
Interest	51.75%*	NIL
Royalties	17.25%**	NIL

* Includes 15% surcharge.
** 10% rate allowed in some cases under investment incentives legislation.

GUERNSEY

There are a number of differences between the tax systems of Guernsey and Jersey, the two largest of the Channel Islands: the Guernsey system applies also to Alderney and Herm, but in Sark there are no income taxes. The Channel Islands are direct dependencies of the British Crown but are not part of the United Kingdom, though the UK is responsible for their foreign relations and defence.

Income tax for individuals and companies is at the low standard rate of 20% and there is no progressive scale of tax for higher incomes. The only form of capital gains tax is a dwelling profits tax, payable by individuals and companies on short-term gains on disposal or leasing of dwellings, but profits from dealing in investments may form part of assessable business profits. There is no value added tax, gift or wealth tax.

There are obvious tax advantages available in Guernsey for companies as well as individuals, but there is a flat-rate corporation tax of £300 per annum on companies which are incorporated in Guernsey but which are not controlled there and do not conduct a substantial part of their activities there. There is partial unilateral relief for double taxation on income from a territory with which Guernsey has no tax treaty.

Guernsey

1 LIST OF TAXES AND LEGISLATION

Individuals and companies:
  Income tax (Income Tax (Guernsey) Law 1975 as amended)
  Dwelling profits tax (Dwelling Profits Tax (Guernsey) Law 1975)
Companies (registered but not resident in Guernsey):
  Corporation tax (Corporation Tax (Guernsey) Law 1950 as amended)

2 INDIVIDUALS' TAXES

(a) *Income charged*
Residents: solely or principally in Guernsey: Income from all sources
Others: Income arising in or received in Guernsey
Non-residents: Income derived from Guernsey

(b) *Year and basis of assessment*
The year of charge is the calendar year. Tax on Guernsey income is computed on the income of the preceding year or, in the case of a business, on that of its accounting year ending in that year ("year of computation") while income from outside Guernsey is assessed on an actual basis.

(c) *Computation of taxable income*
Income from all sources (subject to specified exemptions), less admissible deductions and losses, is assessable. Married couples (unless separated) are jointly assessed. Members of partnerships are individually assessed on their shares of income.

(i) Business or professional income:
Basis
Profits of the preceding year or accounting period, computed on ordinary commercial principles. Contributions to an approved pension scheme for employees are among the admissible deductions. Business losses may be recovered from other income of the year of charge and any amounts not so relieved may be carried forward.

Depreciation allowances
Initial allowances are given only in respect of expenditure on ships, aircraft and glasshouses. Annual allowances are given at rates determined by the Income Tax Authority on these and other assets, including buildings, used for a business.

(ii) Capital gains

A chargeable profit on the sale, or premium on the leasing, of a dwelling (premises used for human habitation) is subject to 100% dwelling profits tax: losses are set off against current or future profits. There are a number of exemptions, e.g. for a dwelling acquired more than a year previously and which has been used as the taxpayer's residence for any continuous period of 12 months, or where the dwelling had been owned for more than 5 years.

Profits on sale of investments are only assessable when the dealings are in the course of a business.

(iii) Special trades etc.

Special provisions apply to investment companies, unit trusts and insurance companies.

(iv) Salaries, wages etc., pensions

All emoluments from office or employment or former employment after deduction of expenses and contributions to approved pension schemes or superannuation funds are taxable. A system of deduction of tax at source from such income was introduced in 1980.

(v) Dividends, interest, etc.

Tax is deductible from dividends and from interest paid by investment companies to non-residents. Dividends paid without deduction of tax are treated as net payments and are grossed up for tax purposes. Bank deposit interest received by non-residents is not taxable unless other income is also derived from Guernsey.

(vi) Income from letting and leasing

The annual rental value of land and buildings owned (unless they are owner-occupied) less standard deductions for repairs and maintenance and for interest paid etc., is assessable.

(vii) Other income

Royalties etc. and any other miscellaneous income other than under (i) – (vi) above are included in taxable income.

(d) Deductions from total income

(i) General deductions

Annual interest paid, not otherwise deductible, and taxes

paid outside Guernsey in the country where income arises (unless double taxation relief is allowed – see 4. below).

(ii) Personal and other allowances
Allowances given to residents include married and single personal allowances and allowances for dependent relatives, earned income etc. Non-resident British nationals in receipt of income from Guernsey may also qualify for proportionate allowances.

(iii) Tax credits
Tax suffered by deduction at source is credited.

(e) Tax deducted at source
(i) Employment income   See (c) (iv) above.
(ii) Dividends, interest etc.   See (c) (v) above.

3 COMPANIES' ETC. TAXES

(a) Types of undertaking charged
All bodies of persons, whether or not incorporated, other than partnerships (see 2.(c) above).

(b) Income charged
Resident companies etc. (i.e. those controlled in Guernsey or incorporated in Guernsey and conducting a substantial part of their activities there): Income from all sources
Foreign companies with a permanent establishment in Guernsey: Income derived from the Guernsey establishment.

(c) Computation of taxable income
The computation of taxable income follows the same general rules as for individuals (2.(c) above) in respect of income tax and dwelling profits tax. Corporation tax, at a flat sum of £300, rather than income tax is levied on every limited liability company which is incorporated in Guernsey but which is not resident (as defined in 3.(b) above) and does not conduct a substantial part of its business from an establishment in Guernsey. See also 2.(c) (iii) above.

4 DOUBLE TAXATION AGREEMENTS

Comprehensive double taxation agreements are in force between Guernsey and the United Kingdom and Jersey. Relief is given to residents for tax on income chargeable both in Guernsey and also in another territory, with which there is no double taxation agreement, at the rate of tax in the other country or three quarters of the effective Guernsey rate, whichever is lower.

5 RATES OF TAX

The rates of income tax are subject to change from year to year, but the sample figures shown below for the year of charge 1983 give an indication of recent rates. Amounts are stated in pounds sterling (£).

(a) Income Tax
The standard rate of income tax ix 20%.
Among the personal reliefs for individuals are:

Personal allowance:	married	Tax on £1,800
	single	Tax on £900
Earned income		Tax on ¼ of net earned income – maximum allowance £500.

There are a number of other allowances, including dependent relatives, wife's earned income, additional personal allowances where income is less than £8,500 for a married person and £4,250 for others. There is also an exemption allowance (the amount varying in accordance with marital status, dependent children and age) and a reduced rate allowance, both given in cases where assessable income does not exceed £8,500 for a married person or £4,250 for others. The tax allowance for children was abolished from 1981, but family allowances were increased to £130 per annum for each child.

(b) Withholding taxes

Payments to non-resident companies:

	General rate	Rate applied under UK double taxation agreement
Dividends	*	*
Interest	20%	20%
Royalties	20%	20%

* Tax deemed to be deducted at the company rate charged on the profits out of which dividends paid – not a true withholding tax.

IRELAND

The Republic of Ireland has inherited many features of its tax system from its long association with the United Kingdom. Ireland is traditionally agricultural, and farm exports, particularly of livestock, are substantial, but the Government has in recent years pursued a policy of industrialisation, and has sought to attract foreign investment by the provision of facilities for new businesses.

Tax incentives available include accelerated depreciation rates for plant, industrial or farm buildings and hotels, and there are regional investment allowances on new plant installed, mainly given for the Western parts of the country. There are also cash grants for new or expanded industrial undertakings in specified less industrialised areas, the grants not being treated as reducing the costs on which capital allowances are given. Companies may qualify for tax exemption on profits from export sales, and complete exemption from corporation tax (known as "Shannon relief") is available for companies established in the airport customs-free area. Manufacturing companies pay a much reduced rate of tax. A further business incentive is afforded by the provisions which have been introduced for tax relief in respect of increases in trading stocks, similar to that given in the United Kingdom.

Personal taxation is on the usual progressive scale but the top rate of 65% is reached at the relatively low level of the excess of taxable income over £IR10,000 (or £IR20,000 for married couples electing joint assessment). Capital gains of all kinds are taxable, subject to initial exemptions, but there are provisions for adjustment to take account of the effects of inflation. An imputation tax system has been in operation since 1976/77 on the introduction of corporation tax. More stringent penalties for tax evasion were introduced in 1983.

Ireland

1 LIST OF TAXES AND LEGISLATION

(i) Income tax: levied on the income of individuals (Income Tax Act 1967).
(ii) Corporation tax: levied on the profits of companies (Corporation Tax Act 1976).
(iii) Capital gains tax (Capital Gains Tax Act 1975).
(iv) Residential Property Tax (Finance Act 1983).

2 TAXATION – INDIVIDUALS

(a) Income charged
Residents: Income and capital gains from all sources
Non-residents: Income and capital gains arising in the Republic.

(b) Year and basis of assessment
The income tax year ends on 5th April: for a business, the year of assessment is its accounting period ending within the preceding tax year.

(c) Computation of taxable income
Married couples are separately assessed unless they elect joint assessment in the name of the husband, who is then entitled to married allowance. Total income less allowances is charged under four Schedules, C, D, E and F, as indicated below.

(i) **Business income** (charged under Sch.D Case I, profits of a trade and Case II, profits of a profession or vocation):
Basis
Net profit of the accounting period ending (except on commencement or cessation of a trade) in the tax year preceding the year of assessment. Profits of a business carried on by a partnership are apportioned to the partners and treated as though arising from separate businesses. There are a number of provisions relating to deductions permissible in computing net profit. A form of stock relief for increase in trading stocks is allowed to businesses engaged in manufacturing, farming and some other trades. Trading losses may be set off against other income or chargeable gains of the year and any amount unrelieved may be carried back to the preceding period or carried forward without time limit.

Ireland

Depreciation allowances
There are provisions for initial and annual allowances, and balancing allowances and charges, in respect of industrial buildings, plant and machinery: "free depreciation" is permitted for new plant and machinery and industrial buildings.

(ii) **Capital gains:**
Gains less losses on disposal of all forms of property, including intangible assets such as goodwill, are chargeable, subject to certain exemptions and reliefs: "disposal" includes gifts but not transfer on death, which is subject to capital acquisitions tax. There are provisions for adjusting capital gains and capital gains tax for inflation.
A residential property tax, introduced in 1983, provides for a tax of 1½% on the excess of current market value over £IR65,000 of properties owned and occupied by a taxpayer, subject to certain reliefs based on income. Persons not domiciled in Ireland are liable only on property in Ireland.

(iii) **Special trades, professions etc.**
Export trade businesses may have temporary relief from tax under certain conditions if export sales exceed the sales made in a standard period. Special provisions apply to farming, banks and insurance. There are a number of special exemptions from tax including e.g. (a) profits of authors, composers, artists etc. resident in the Republic from work of cultural or artistic merit, (b) gains from commercial woodlands in the Republic, (c) patent royalties to residents in the Republic arising from work carried out in the Republic.

(iv) **Salaries, wages etc., pensions**
The charge is under Sch.E. Income from all kinds of employment and former employment is chargeable, including benefits in kind and expense allowances, and compensation payments in certain cases: approved retirement benefit payments and other expenses are deductible: tax is deducted at source under a PAYE system. A special Sch. E allowance of £IR600 is deductible to compensate for tax being paid currently under PAYE, rather than in arrears.

(v) Dividends, interest etc.

The charge is under Sch.C for certain interest etc. paid out of public revenue and under Sch.D Case III in other instances: tax assessed under Case III is normally on a preceding year basis. Tax is deducted at source at the standard rate from interest paid under Sch.C: annual interest is mostly paid gross, but interest paid by a company or paid to a non-resident is subject to tax deduction. Dividends are subject to a tax credit on an imputation system. There are some special reliefs, including dividends paid by Irish companies to Irish residents on capital raised for industrial expansion in the Republic.

(vi) Income from letting and leasing

Rents received, less expenses, are normally assessed under Sch.D Case V on the preceding year basis: tax on the gross amount is deducted at source from payments to non-residents.

(vii) Other income

Profits and gains not assessed under any other provision may be charged under Sch.D Case IV.

(d) Deductions from total income

(i) General deductions

Relief is given for medical insurance payments, for home improvements, for bank etc. interest payable in the Republic within limits and for life assurance premiums. Relief is no longer allowed for interest on new personal loans, other than on the borrower's principal residence, and relief for interest on existing loans ceases in 1985.

(ii) Personal and other allowances

There is relief *inter alia* for personal allowances (married and single), age allowance, working wife allowance, child allowance, housekeeper and dependent relative allowances. A special employee allowance is given where income includes emoluments taxed under the PAYE system.

(iii) Tax credits

Credit is given for tax suffered by deduction at source.

Ireland

(e) **Tax deducted at source**

(i) Employment income
See (c) (iv) above: PAYE system in force.

(ii) Interest
See (c) (v) above.

3 CORPORATION TAX – COMPANIES

(a) Types of undertaking charged
Any body corporate, subject to certain exemptions.

(b) Income charged
Resident companies: Profits from all sources
Non-resident companies: Profits arising in the Republic

(c) Computation of taxable income

(i) Basis
Total net profit (before payment of any dividends) arising in the accounting period ending within the tax year is taxable income. The computation and exemptions are in the main as for individuals (see 2(c) (i) above). Dividends (plus tax credits) received by one resident company from another are treated as "franked investment income".
Special tax incentives include:
(a) Shannon relief: tax exemption for approved trades carried on in the airport customs-free area.
(b) Export relief: exemption or relief in the early years up to 1990 for new or increased exports of Irish manufactured goods.
(c) Manufacturing industry: the general rate of tax is reduced to 10%, or less for "small companies".
"Advance corporation tax" payments are required since 1983, amounting to the difference between the tax credits on distributions made and received. As a transitional measure, ACT is only payable at 50% on distributions up to 31 December 1984.

(ii) Capital gains
Chargeable capital gains are subject to corporation tax, but at the same effective rates and the same general method of computation as for the capital gains of individuals.

4 DOUBLE TAXATION AGREEMENTS

General agreements on income and profits are in force between the Republic of Ireland and the United Kingdom as well as 18 other countries. The agreement with the United Kingdom covers income tax, corporation tax and capital gains tax and provision is made for the treatment of "double residents" (resident in both countries).

5 RATES OF TAX

The rates of tax are subject to change from year to year, but the samples shown below for 1983-84 give some indication of recent rates. Amounts are stated in Irish pounds (£IR).

(a) Individual

There are separate scales of tax on taxable income for jointly assessed married couples (see 2(c) above) and others:

		Married couples	*Others*
Reduced rate	25% on first	£IR2,000	£IR1,000
Standard rate	35% on next	£IR6,000	£IR3,000
Higher rates	45% on next	£IR4,000	£IR2,000
	55% on next	£IR4,000	£IR2,000
	60% on next	£IR4,000	£IR2,000
	65% on over	£IR20,000	£IR10,000

Small incomes are however exempted (single £IR2,400, married £IR4,800, with increases for age).

Allowances given in computing taxable income include:

Personal reliefs: Jointly assessed married couples £IR2,900
Others £IR1,450
Children (each) £IR100
(if incapacitated £IR500)
Employee allowance £IR600

In the 1984 Budget, the 25% reduced rate is abolished, the slice of income affected being charged at 35% for 1984/85. Some allowances have however been increased.

(b) Companies corporation tax

Rates of tax on taxable profits:
Full rate 50%
Capital gains: see (c) below

Ireland

Manufacturing profits (further reduced for
    "small companies")   10%
Small companies (profits not over £IR25,000)   40%
Special reduced rate (public utilities and
    some other companies)   35%

(c) Capital gains tax

Rate of tax on chargeable gains (individuals and companies):
    General rate   40%
    Assets held one year or less   60%
    "   " 1 - 3 years   50%
Residential property tax – see 2(c)(ii) above.

(d) Withholding taxes

Payments to non-resident companies:

	General rate	Rate applied under UK double taxation agreement
Dividends (imputation system)	NIL	NIL*
Interest	35%	NIL
Royalties	35%	NIL

*A UK resident company with less than a 10% interest in the paying company is entitled to receive the tax credit of 35/65ths of the dividend less Irish tax at 15%.

ISLE OF MAN

The small territory of the Isle of Man in the Irish Sea has its own administration and laws, with taxation separate from that of the United Kingdom. The island has a very ancient form of assembly, the Tynwald, which fixes the rates of tax annually.

The Manx economy relies much on the tourist industry, but there are tax advantages to attract outsiders for residence or business purposes and tax concessions are available to persons carrying out beneficial industrial development. There is a flat-rate £250 tax per annum on companies registered in the Isle of Man but not controlled or carrying on business there.

The standard rate of income tax for individuals and companies is at the low rate of 20% and there is no progressive scale for higher levels of income. There is no general taxation of capital gains, but there is a land speculation tax, at the standard rate of income tax, on relatively short-term profits on sale of land in the island, unless it has been used for a business by a resident.

Tax at the standard rate is deductible from payments of income to non-residents. There is a double taxation agreement with the United Kingdom and unilateral relief is available for residents on income from other countries.

Isle of Man

1 LIST OF TAXES AND LEGISLATION

(i) Income tax:
Levied on the income of individuals and companies etc.
(Income Tax Act 1970, as subsequently amended).

(ii) Land Speculation Tax (not further dealt with in this summary):
Levied on individuals and companies, at the standard rate of income tax, on profit from the sale of land in the Isle of Man, subject to a number of exemptions, e.g. land held for 5 years, dwelling house owned and occupied for 3 years, land used for a business by a resident (Land Speculation Tax Act 1974).

2 INDIVIDUALS' INCOME TAX

(a) Income charged
Residents (including temporary residents actually resident 6 months in year of assessment): Income from all sources
Non-residents: Income arising or accruing in the Isle of Man.

(b) Year and basis of assessment
Income tax is levied for the year of assessment ending on April 5th on the taxable income for the preceding year to April 5th.

(c) Computation of taxable income
Taxable income is the total income (subject to exemptions) less admissible deductions for expenses wholly and exclusively incurred for the purpose of acquiring the income and for personal reliefs, and after set-off for losses. Married persons are normally jointly assessed. Members of partnerships are individually assessed on their shares of income.

(i) Business or professional income:
Basis
Taxable income of the preceding year. A person carrying out an industrial development certified as beneficial to the Isle of Man may be granted tax remissions or concessions. Contributions to an approved retirement benefit scheme, established in connection with a trade etc. carried on in the Isle of Man by a resident, are admissible deductions and the income of such a fund is exempt from tax.

Depreciation allowances
Initial and annual allowances are computed in the same way as for United Kingdom tax. On premises for the lodging of tourists the initial allowance is 15% and annual allowance 2½%.

(ii) Capital gains
There is no provision for income tax on capital gains (but see 1.(ii) above regarding Land Speculation Tax).

(iii) Special trades etc.
Special provisions apply to insurance companies.

(iv) Salaries, wages etc., pensions
Income from employment and former employment is assessable, including accommodation or other benefits provided. Contributions to approved retirement benefit schemes etc., are admissible deductions. Instalment payments of tax are deducted from remuneration by employers in accordance with tax tables.

(v) Dividends, interest etc.
Dividends, interest etc. are included in taxable income. The payers may be required to deduct tax from payments to non-residents.

(vi) Income from letting and leasing
In computing income from rents a fixed deduction is allowed for repairs and expenses. The payers may be required to deduct tax from payments to non-residents.

(d) Deductions from total income

(i) General deductions
Life assurance relief at 10% of premiums is available to residents within certain limits. Unrecovered losses brought forward are deductible.

(ii) Personal and other allowances
Personal reliefs given to individual residents include allowances for earned income, children and dependants, married and single personal allowances.

(iii) Tax credits
Credit is given for tax deducted at source, instalment

payments deducted from employment income and double taxation relief.

(e) Tax deducted at source

(i) Employment income (instalment payments):
See (c) (iv) above.
(ii) Dividends, interest etc.   See (c) (v) above.
(iii)Rents etc.   See (c) (vi) above.

3   COMPANIES' INCOME TAX

(a) Types of undertaking charged
Associations other than partnerships: namely, any company corporate or unincorporate, fraternity, fellowship, society or association of persons.

(b) Income charged
Resident companies etc.: Income from all sources
Non-resident companies etc.: Income arising or accruing in the Isle of Man.

(c) Computation of taxable income
The computation is in the main in accordance with the same rules as for individuals. Dividends and other distributions by resident companies etc., registered in the Isle of Man are deductible in computing their taxable income. Provisions for group relief were made in the Income Tax Act 1980. An annual registration tax of £250 is levied on a company incorporated in the Isle of Man but not carrying on a business there and controlled from outside the Isle of Man.

4   DOUBLE TAXATION

There is a double taxation agreement between the Isle of Man and the United Kingdom, under which credit is allowed to a person resident in the Isle of Man for the year of assessment. Unilateral relief is given to Isle of Man residents for income chargeable to tax both there and in another country (if the foreign tax corresponds with Manx income tax) at the effective rate of Manx or foreign tax, whichever is lower.

5   RATES OF TAX

The effective rates of income tax are subject to change from year to year, but the samples shown below for the year of assessment 1984-85 give an indication of recent rates. Amounts are stated in sterling.

(a) Individuals

Standard rate of tax (residents and non-residents)   20%
Exemption limits for aged persons:
  Married man   £4,540 income
  Single person   £2,653 income
Personal reliefs include:
  Earned income   25% (maximum £1,550)
  Personal allowance:
    married   £2,880
    single   £1,690
  Children's, dependants' and other allowances.

(b) Companies etc.

Standard rate of tax (resident and non-resident)   20%

(c) Withholding taxes

Payments to non-resident companies:

	General rate	Rate applied under UK double taxation agreement
Dividends	20%	20%
Interest	20%	20%
Royalties	20%	20%

ITALY

A number of tax reforms were introduced in Italy in 1973-74 which resulted in some simplification of the tax system. When these were introduced, there was provision for an amnesty for unsettled earlier claims which were dealt with by calculations on a compromise basis, and there has been a further amnesty law in 1982.

Italy now has national income taxes and in addition there are local taxes. The local taxes on income levied on behalf of municipalities and other authorities are now at a unified total rate in place of the varying rates previously separately calculated: they do not apply to employment or dividend income. A tax on capital appreciation of real property is levied by the State on behalf of the municipality in which the property is situated, the rates varying within a specified range. There is no general wealth tax.

The national income tax payable by individuals is on a highly progressive scale but the top rates are only reached at a very high level of income. The standard rate of corporate income tax is comparatively low at 30%, but local income tax is payable in addition.

There are tax incentives in various forms for investments in certain areas such as the Mezzogiorno where development is encouraged.

Some kinds of capital gain are taxable, including gains on "speculative transactions" from land development and from certain relatively short-term disposals: there is however no general provision for the taxation of gains on realisation of investments, for instance, unless they are included in business assets.

There is a comprehensive system for withholding of taxes from payments of income to non-residents.

1 LIST OF TAXES AND LEGISLATION

The decrees quoted are the basic legislation but they are subject to subsequent amendments. Rules as to procedure, reliefs and collection of taxes are contained in Decrees Nos. 600 – 602 of 29 September 1973.

(a) National taxes
  (i) Individual income tax *(Imposta sul reddito delle persone fisiche):* Decree No. 597 of 29 September 1973
    A tax imputation system was introduced in 1977, applicable to resident shareholders.
  (ii) Corporate income tax *(Imposta sul reddito delle persone giuridiche):* Decree No. 598 of 29 September 1973

(b) Local taxes (not further dealt with in this summary)
  (i) Local income tax *(Imposta locale sui redditi):* Decree No. 599 of 29 September 1973
    This tax is levied by local authorities on individuals and companies etc. in respect of income produced in their district, other than income
    (a) from employment,
    (b) from holdings in companies etc. (subject to corporate income tax), or
    (c) subject to a withholding tax.
    A number of deductions, exemptions and reliefs are allowed. Rates of tax have now been unified at a total of 15% for municipalities and other authorities, with a temporary surcharge of 8%. The tax is deductible from income for the national income tax.

  (ii) Tax on capital appreciation of real property *(Imposta comunale sull'incremento di valore degli immobili):* Decree No. 643 of 26 October 1972
    This tax is levied by the state on behalf of the municipalities where the property is situated. It is chargeable on the increase in value of real property, or the right thereto, on disposal for consideration and on acquisition without consideration, e.g. by inheritance: it is also chargeable at ten year intervals on properties owned by property companies. Subject to certain exemptions and allowances, the taxable appreciation is based on the increase in value

since acquisition. The rate of tax is fixed by the municipality within specified limits, with a range of rates increasing progressively, according to the ratio of appreciation, from a minimum of 3% to a maximum of 30% on appreciation of over 200% on cost multiplied by the number of years of ownership.

2 INCOME TAX – INDIVIDUALS

(a) Income charged
Residents: World wide income
Non-residents: Income from Italian sources.

(b) Year and basis of assessment
The tax year is the calendar year.

(c) Computation of taxable income
Tax is calculated on the total net income of the taxpayer. Married persons are each separately assessed on personal income plus half the income of their minor children. Some classes of income are excluded from the basic charge and taxed separately. Members of partnerships are individually liable for tax on their shares of income.

(i) Business income:
Basis
Net profit of the tax period (calendar year) is chargeable, deductions allowed in the computation being specified. Permissible methods of valuing stocks are stated. Small businesses are permitted to keep simplified accounts. Losses may be carried forward for 5 years.

Depreciation allowances
A straight-line method is used, maximum rates being specified. Small amounts may be written off in full. The maximum annual allowance for intangible assets, such as patents, trade marks and goodwill, is 20% of cost.

(ii) Capital gains:
Disposal of business
Gains are charged separately at the average rate applicable to aggregate income for the previous two years.

Business assets
Gains are included in business income.

"Speculative transactions"
Gains on the development of land and on the realisation within 5 years of purchase of real property not intended for personal use, and within 2 years of purchase of antiques etc., are charged after deduction of any tax on capital appreciation (see 1. (b) (ii) above).

Exempt gains
There is no general provision for taxation of any gains other than the above (e.g. on realisation of investments not included in business assets).

(iii) Agricultural and professional activities

Taxable income from agriculture is a notional income determined in accordance with official valuation schedules. Income from professional activities, patent etc. royalties and some other types of independent work is taxable after specified deductions (including e.g. working expenses).

(iv) Salaries, wages etc., pensions

Net income from all kinds of employment and former employment, and also from some other sources, e.g. annuities and alimony which do not qualify for earned income allowance, is taxable. Instead of deducting actual expenses, a taxpayer may elect to have a credit of L.18,000 deducted from the tax on employment income. Tax is withheld at source from income of this nature.

(v) Dividends, interest etc.

Taxable income from capital, including dividends and interest, and also gains from lotteries, gambling etc. is chargeable: net dividends to residents are subject to tax credit of ⅓rd under the tax imputation system.

(vi) Income from letting and leasing

Notional income from ownership of farm land and of permanent buildings in Italy, based on official valuation schedules and subject to certain allowances for expenses, is taxable.

(vii) Other income
Taxable income includes income from occasional activities, from leasing of movable property, or from real property outside Italy (no deduction being allowed for foreign tax).

(d) Deductions from total income

(i) General deductions
Aggregate income is reduced by local income tax, social security etc. contributions, life insurance premiums and some other expenses.

(ii) Personal allowances
Fixed allowances (tax credits) are given for single and married taxpayers and for dependants (including children) and also in respect of earned income from employment and from pensions. Non-residents are not entitled to personal allowances, except that they receive a tax credit of L.240,000 in respect of employment income or pension from Italy.

(e) Tax deducted at source

(i) Employment income
See (c) (iv) above: tax deducted is treated as advance payment of income tax. A final withholding tax at 20% is deducted from payments to non-residents of fees for professional and other independent activities.

(ii) Interest etc.
A general rate of deduction of 20% is applied, with lower rates in some cases, but with an 8% surcharge.

(iii) Dividends etc.
Varying rates are applied, including final withholding tax at 30% from payments to non-residents, subject to part repayment where foreign tax is suffered: there is a surcharge of 8% on payments to non-residents.

3 INCOME TAX – COMPANIES ETC.

(a) Types of undertaking charged
Public limited companies (le società per azioni)

Private limited companies *(le società a responsibilità limitata)*
Limited partnerships
Other kinds of partnership.

(b) Income charged

Limited companies and limited partnerships having their administrative headquarters or main business in Italy: World wide income from all sources

Non-resident entities as above: Income from Italian sources

Certain kinds of partnerships are subject to individual income tax attributed to individual partners.

(c) Computation of taxable income

(i) Basis

Computed in the main as for individuals (see 2(c) (i) above), the tax period being the accounting period of the concern: capital gains credited to a special reserve and re-invested in depreciable assets within 2 years are not taxable, but the gains are transferred to accumulated depreciation on the assets acquired. Local income tax paid is deductible. A tax credit of 42.85% is given on dividends received by one resident company from another.

(ii) Capital gains

In general as for an individual (see 2(c) (ii) above).

(iii) Dividends, interest etc.

As for an individual, but treated as business income (see 2(c) (v) above).

(iv) Letting and leasing

As for an individual, but treated as business income (see 2(c) (vi) above).

4   DOUBLE TAXATION AGREEMENTS

General agreements on income and profits are in force between Italy and the United Kingdom, as well as over 30 other countries. Where a gross amount of foreign income, arising in a country with which Italy has a double taxation agreement, is included in the computation, credit is allowed for the foreign tax of not less than 25% nor more than 66⅔% of the attributable Italian tax. Where income arises in a country which does not allow such relief, credit may be given for the foreign tax not exceeding 25% of the attributable Italian tax.

5   RATES OF TAX

The rates of tax are subject to change from year to year, but the samples shown below for 1983 give some indication of recent rates. Amounts are quoted in Lire (L).

(a) Individuals' income tax

The rates of tax on successive slices of taxable income range from 18% on up to L.11 million to 41% on L.39 million – L.60 million and 65% on over L.500 million.

Allowances (tax credits) for residents deducted from the calculated tax include:

Personal allowance	L.36,000
Married person	L.240,000 (if spouse's taxable income does not exceed L.2,750,000)
Dependent children	increasing from L.18,000 for one to L.228,000 for each one over eight: each spouse is entitled to the deduction, and if one has taxable income not over L.2,750,000, the other may deduct double the amount
Earned income allowance	person in employment L.252,000

Further allowances are given for small incomes, for other dependants and also in respect of expenses. For non-residents see 2(d)(ii) above.

(b) Companies etc. income tax

General rate   30%

The rate for 1984 is increased to 36%, making an effective rate of national and local tax combined of approximately 46.4%.

(c) *Withholding taxes*

Payments to non-resident companies:

	General rate	*Rate applied under UK double taxation agreement*
Dividends	32.4%	5% or 15%*
Interest	16.2% or 21.6%**	16.2% or 21.6%**
Royalties	21%	NIL

* The lower rate to a company owning 51% or more of voting power: surcharge of 8%, not applicable under UK double taxation agreement.

** The lower rate on loan interest: 8% surcharge included.

JERSEY

Jersey in the Channel Islands has a taxation system separate from, but bearing a number of resemblances to, that of the main part of the United Kingdom. Non-resident British subjects with income derived from Jersey are, unlike other non-residents, entitled to proportional personal reliefs and the reduced rate for the first £250 of taxable income: there is also partial relief for double taxation on pensions received from other parts of the Commonwealth and South Africa.

The single tax on income of both individuals and companies is the income tax. This is a low-rate tax of 20%, subject to an initial reduced rate for individuals and with quite a high exemption limit, particularly for persons with dependent children. There is no progressive scale for the higher ranges of income and no provision for the taxation of capital gains other than those accruing in the course of a business. Doubtless because of the attraction to external companies of the favourable taxation position, there is a flat rate corporation tax of £300 per annum payable by externally controlled companies registered in Jersey.

1 LIST OF TAXES AND LEGISLATION

(a) Income tax
Levied on the income of individuals and companies, under the Income Tax (Jersey) Law 1961, as subsequently amended.

(b) Corporation tax (not further dealt with in this summary)
A flat rate tax of £300 per annum on limited liability companies registered in Jersey but not controlled there: a company is exempt from the tax for a year for which it elects to be assessed to income tax (Corporation Tax (Jersey) Law 1956).

2 INDIVIDUALS' INCOME TAX

(a) Income charged
Residents ordinarily resident: Income from all sources
Non-residents (including persons not ordinarily resident): Income derived from or received in Jersey.

(b) Year and basis of assessment
The year of assessment ends on December 31st or on the normal accounting date of a business. Income is classified under three schedules for the purpose of assessment:

Schedule A :ownership of land, buildings etc. in Jersey, charged on a current year basis.

Schedule C :interest and dividends payable from public sources or by coupon, tax being deducted at source.

Schedule D :other income, divided into 6 cases (I – VI): income from a trade, profession etc. is assessed on a preceding year basis and other income on a current year basis.

(c) Computation of taxable income
Total income less exemptions and admissible deductions and after set-off of losses is chargeable. Married persons are normally jointly assessed. Partnerships are jointly assessed but individual partners may claim deductions from their shares of income for losses, personal allowances etc. to which they may be entitled.

    (i) **Business or professional income:**
    Basis
    Net profit of a trade (including agriculture) is assessed

under Sch.D Case I and income from a profession etc. under Case II (in both instances only if carried on in Jersey, otherwise under Case V): a preceding year basis is used. Admissible deductions include expenses wholly and exclusively incurred for the purpose of the trade, profession etc., and also the annual value, assessed under Sch.A, of any property occupied for the purpose of the trade etc. Losses on one trade etc. may be deducted from profits for the same year of another trade, or carried forward and deducted from the profits of the same trade in a subsequent year.

Depreciation allowances
A deduction is allowed of a reasonable amount for wear and tear of plant and machinery, including glasshouses.

(ii) **Capital gains**
There is no provision for taxing capital gains, but dealing profits on the sale of assets in the course of a business may be assessable.

(iii) **Special trades**
Special provisions apply to insurance companies, investment companies and savings banks.

(iv) **Salaries, wages etc., pensions**
Income from employment or former employment is assessed, if it is derived from Jersey, under Sch.D Case II, and otherwise under Case V. A deduction is allowed for expenses incurred in producing the income, including wear and tear allowances, where applicable, and contributions to approved superannuation funds. There is no PAYE system.

(v) **Dividends, interest etc.**
Tax is deductible at source from dividend and interest payments. Bank deposit interest received by non-residents is not taxable unless other income is also derived from Jersey.

(vi) **Income from letting and leasing**
Tax under Sch.A is payable by the owner on the annual value of property (unless it is unoccupied or, from 1983, owner-occupied) less an allowance for repairs.

(vii) Other income
Tax is payable on all annual profits and gains which are not specifically exempted.

(d) Deductions from total income

(i) General deductions
Life assurance and deferred annuity premiums are, within limits, admissible deductions.

(ii) Personal and other allowances
Personal reliefs include those for earned income, married and single personal allowances, children and dependants.

(iii) Tax credits
Tax credit is given for double taxation where applicable and for tax suffered by deduction at source.

(e) Tax deducted at source

(i) Dividends, interest etc.
See (c) (v) above.

(ii) Miscellaneous
Tax is deductible from annual payments for royalties, annuities and certain charges on property.

3 COMPANIES' INCOME TAX

(a) Types of undertaking charged
Companies wherever incorporated or registered.

(b) Income charged
As for individuals (see 2.(a) above).

(c) Computation of taxable income
The computation of taxable income is in accordance with the same rules as for individuals, so far as applicable. The income of approved superannuation funds and pension schemes is exempt, and tax on annuities paid by them to residents may be assessed on the recipient under Sch.D Case VI rather than be deducted at source.

4 DOUBLE TAXATION

Comprehensive double taxation agreements are in force between Jersey and the United Kingdom and Guernsey, relief being available only to residents. Pensions subjected to tax in a Commonwealth country or South Africa are charged at one half of the Jersey rate payable on the recipients' taxable income. Unilateral relief is given for double taxation in other cases by treating foreign tax as an expense deducted from income.

5   RATES OF TAX

The rates of tax are subject to change from year to year, but the samples shown below for the year of assessment 1983 give an indication of recent rates. Amounts are stated in sterling (£).

(a) Individuals

The standard rate of income tax is 20%, subject to a small reduced rate band, and there is an exemption limit (increased by £950 for each dependent child) of £4,950 for married persons and £3,400 for others.

Personal reliefs, available to residents and (with certain restrictions) to non-resident British subjects, include:

Earned income	25% (maximum £1,850)
Personal allowance:	
married	£1,700
single	£850
Children (each)	£950

Dependants, age, wife's earned income etc.

(b) Companies

The standard rate of income tax is 20%.

(c) Withholding taxes

Payments to non-resident companies:

	General rate	Rate applied under UK double taxation agreement
Dividends	*	*
Interest	20%	20%
Royalties	20%	20%

* Tax deemed to be deducted at the company rate charged on the profits out of which dividends paid – not a true withholding tax.

LUXEMBOURG

The tax system of Luxembourg is based on State taxes on income together with the capital tax, which is a form of wealth tax, and local taxes on businesses and on the ownership of real property: there are in addition surcharges for the unemployment fund and a national investment levy.

Capital gains are taxable in a number of different forms. Gains on sale of business assets are treated as income from trade. For an individual, the taxability of gains on the disposal of land or buildings depends on the length of ownership, but a gain from sale of the taxpayer's principal residence is exempt: gains on most other assets held for over six months are exempt, but special provisions apply to realisation of shareholdings of over 25% in a company.

There are somewhat complicated arrangements for the allocation of taxpayers to Groups (depending on marital status and dependent children), allowances being given by modifications of the basic tax scale varying for each group. This results in a considerable smoothing of the graduation of rates for married and elderly taxpayers and for those with dependants.

Several different kinds of tax incentive are available for businesses, consisting of investment allowances on purchases of some kinds of fixed asset (other than real property, livestock etc.) and tax reliefs on the establishment of approved new industrial enterprises.

There is a full system of withholding taxes deducted from income paid to non-residents.

Luxembourg

1 LIST OF TAXES AND LEGISLATION

The income taxes are governed by the Income Tax Law of 4 December 1967, as subsequently amended.

(a) National taxes on income

(i) Income Tax *(Impôt sur le Revenu/Einkommensteuer):* levied on the income of individuals.

(ii) Directors' Tax *(Retenue d'impôt sur les Tantièmes/ Steuerabzug von Aufsichtsratsvergütungen):* deducted at source from directors' fees.

(iii)Corporation Tax *(Impôt sur le Revenu des Collectivités/ Körperschaftsteuer):* levied on the profits of companies and other associations.

(iv)National Investment Levy *(Contribution nationale d'investissement)*: levied on the profits of self-employed professional people.

(b) Other taxes (not further dealt with in this summary)

(i) Capital Tax *(Impôt sur la Fortune/Vermögensteuer)*: a wealth tax charged on the capital of individuals and companies (other than holding companies) subject to exemptions (e.g. domestic effects). There are personal allowances for individuals (100,000F plus 100,000F for a wife and 100,000F for each dependent child). The tax is at ½% per annum, subject to a minimum tax of 2,500F for public companies and 1,000F for private companies. Residents are charged on total capital, non-residents on capital in Luxembourg: the tax is not deductible in computing taxable income.

(ii) Business Tax: a communal tax on businesses etc., composed of taxes on profit, business capital and payroll, at varying rates between 5.6% and 12%: the tax is deductible in computing national taxable income.

(iii)Real Property Tax: a communal tax at varying rates up to about 6% on the capital value of real property, the higher rates being on business property: the tax is deductible in computing income and corporation taxes.

2 INDIVIDUALS' TAXATION

(a) Income charged
Residents: Income from all sources
Non-residents: Income arising in Luxembourg

(b) Year and basis of assessment
The tax year is the calendar year or, for a business for which proper accounts are kept, may be its accounting year, subject to prior approval. The normal business year for foresters ends on September 30th.

(c) Computation of taxable income
Taxable income is the total of eight categories of income from trade, farming and forestry, independent work, employment, pensions and annuities, capital, letting and leasing, and other income: in each case losses and the costs of acquiring the income are deducted, and certain special expenses and personal reliefs are deductible from total net income (see (d) below). Quarterly advance payments on account are required, based on the assessment for the previous year. Married persons, unless separated, are jointly assessed. Members of partnerships and of companies in which they may be regarded as entrepreneurs are personally liable for tax on their shares of profit.

(i) Business or professional income:
Basis
Income from trade and income from independent work (self-employment) are treated as separate categories, but the computation of profits for both is on similar lines. Profit is normally computed as the difference between business capital at the beginning and end of the year, after adjusting for withdrawals and new investment in the year, but in some cases a simplified basis of receipts less expenditure may be permitted. Provision is made for investment credits to be set off against tax (or carried forward for up to 4 years), based on purchases of new assets, other than buildings, livestock, mineral deposits etc.: the calculation is as follows:
1. A credit of 12% of the amount of "supplementary investment" in qualifying assets.

2. A credit of 6% up to 6,000,000F and 2% thereafter on purchases of assets with a depreciation life of not less than 8 years.

There is also an allowance, subject to certain conditions, to taxpayers establishing approved new industrial enterprises helpful to the Luxembourg economy: a deduction is allowed of 25% of the profit from the new enterprise (subject to a number of restrictions) for the first 8 years of operation.

Depreciation allowances
Depreciation of buildings and other fixed assets is allowed at rates based on their useful working life. A law of 1982 provided for the revaluation of fixed assets with tax allowances on the revised values.

(ii) **Capital gains**
Capital gains on sale of a business or business assets are treated as income from trade: similar provisions apply to gains in connection with farming, forestry or independent professional work. Included under the category of "other income" are:

1. Capital gains from sales of shareholdings in companies in which the taxpayer has held an interest of over 25%.
2. Gains arising on sale of real property (other than the taxpayer's principal residence) within 2 years of acquisition, or of other assets within 6 months of acquisition.
3. Gains on disposal between 2 and 10 years after acquisition of real property other than the taxpayer's principal residence.
4. Gains on disposal more than 10 years after acquisition of building land.

There is an abatement of 1,250,000F against the total of gains under 1., 3. and 4. above once in each 10 year period, and these gains are taxed at a special rate of half the rate applicable to global income, with a maximum of 28.5%. "Speculative" gains under 2. above are taxed at the full rate. Capital losses not recovered against gains of the year are not carried forward.

(iii) Special trades

Income from farming and forestry is treated as a separate category of income. Some special provisions apply, but in the main the computation of income and capital gains is as for a trade. There is a special investment allowance for expenditure on productive machinery, conversion of cowsheds etc.

(iv) Salaries, wages etc., pensions

Income from employment and income from pensions and annuities are separate categories. All kinds of income from employment (other than the directors' fees referred to below) and from former employment, including benefits in kind, are assessable subject to certain specified exemptions. There is a deduction for the costs of acquisition of employment income (minimum 25,000F, and more if substantiated). A further "compensatory abatement" may be deducted both from employment income (up to 18,000F, but not exceeding the difference between gross income and the deductions for acquisition costs as above and for special expenses – see (d) (i) below) and also from employment pension income (varying between 18,000F and 24,000F as a maximum). A wife with income from employment is entitled to the same deductions. A withholding tax is deducted at source in accordance with an official scale.

Fees paid to resident directors by resident companies are subject to directors' tax at 25%: this is not part of the income tax and cannot be credited against assessed income tax, but net fees after deduction of directors' tax are included in total income for income tax purposes. Directors' tax at 25% and income tax at 8.66% are withheld from the fees of non-resident directors: if the fees do not exceed 53,000F per annum, the tax liability is deemed to be satisfied thereby.

(v) Dividends, interest etc.

Dividends and other distributions by companies and interest are assessed in the category of income from capital. The first 60,000F of savings deposit and government bond interest is exempt. A standard deduction of

1,000F, or more if substantiated, is given for costs of acquisition of the income. Capital yields tax at 15% is deducted at source from interest on profit-sharing bonds but there is no withholding tax on other kinds of interest.

(vi) Income from letting and leasing
Included in this category of income is that derived from letting of real property and other assets and also copyright and patent royalties. Tax is withheld at source from royalty payments to non-residents. The rental value of the taxpayer's residence is included as income.

(vii) Other income
Miscellaneous taxable income may include that derived from sources such as occasional services: income of this sort of less than 10,000F in a year is ignored.

(d) Deductions from total income

(i) General deductions
Admissible deductions by residents include special expenses such as loan interest, pension contributions and social security contributions: a standard deduction of 18,000F is given for such expenses, other than social security contributions, unless a larger amount can be substantiated. A wife with earned income is entitled to the same allowance. In general, unrecovered business losses of the previous 5 years may be deducted: since 1981 however businesses in an economic sector declared to be in a 'structural crisis' have been allowed to carry forward indefinitely 50% of depreciation allowances due for a period in which a tax loss is incurred.

(ii) Personal and other allowances
Taxpayers are divided into three groups as follows:

Group I   Single taxpayers not in other groups
Group II   Unless they qualify for Group III, married persons, taxpayers over 65 years of age and some others
Group III   Taxpayers entitled to child allowance

The basic rates of tax are modified in accordance with separate rules for each group (see 5. below). In addition to the reliefs provided by allocation to a particular group, an extraordinary burdens relief is given for taxpayers who necessarily bear greater expenditure than normal for their status, as for instance handicapped or disabled persons.

Non-residents assessed to tax are charged under Group II but tax must be at least 15% of the income assessed, plus the unemployment fund surcharge (see 5(a) below).

(iii) Tax credits
Credit is given against the total liability for tax deducted at source (other than directors' tax – see (c) (iv) above), for relief under double taxation agreements, and for foreign income taxes not covered by double taxation agreements.

(e) Tax deducted at source
In addition to the regulations referred to below, the revenue authorities may if necessary deduct tax at source from payments to non-residents of income not normally treated in this way.

(i) Employment income   See (c) (iv) above.
(ii) Dividends, interest etc.   See (c) (v) above.
(iii)Royalties   See (c) (vi) above.

3 CORPORATION TAX

(a) Types of undertaking charged
Public and private limited companies
Limited partnerships with share capital
Other associations possessing legal personality.

(b) Income charged
Resident companies (i.e. those incorporated under Luxembourg law or whose head office or administration are in Luxembourg): Income from all sources
Non-resident companies: Income arising in Luxembourg.

(c) Computation of taxable income
The computation for corporation tax is in general in accordance with the same rules as for income tax on individuals, so far as applicable, but all income received by a company (including capital gains) is treated as business income. The

Luxembourg

remuneration of directors is not an admissible deduction in computing taxable income. Resident companies are exempt from tax on dividends received from companies in which they have a holding of 25% or more.

All holding companies with paid-up capital over a prescribed minimum, which do not themselves engage in any industrial or commercial activity and do not have a business establishment in Luxembourg, are exempt from corporation tax but are subject to a capital contribution duty and other special taxes.

4 DOUBLE TAXATION

Comprehensive double taxation agreements are in force between Luxembourg and the United Kingdom and also about 10 other countries.

5 RATES OF TAX

The rates of tax are subject to change from year to year, but the sample figures shown below for the year 1984 give an indication of recent rates. Amounts are stated in Luxembourg francs (F).

(a) Individuals

The basic income tax scale is graduated on successive slices of taxable income rising, after nil on the first 117,600F, to 12% on the next 13,200F, 30% on 370,201 – 416,400F, and 57% on the balance over 1,266,600F. The basic scale is modified as follows for the three groups referred to at 2(d) (ii) above:

Group I The basic scale applies after a deduction, for taxable income not over 267,600F, of 1/5th of the difference between 267,600F and the taxable income.

Group II Tax is charged on half the taxable income at the rates shown in the basic scale; the result is then multiplied by 2.

Group III (i) For taxpayers with taxable income not exceeding 685,200F a "family part" system is applied, depending on the number of dependent children, the "parts" being for one child 2.6, for two 3.4 and for three 4.6. Tax is computed at basic scale rates on taxable income divided by the number of "parts": the resulting amount of tax is then multiplied by the number of "parts" and a surcharge for the unemployment fund is added, at 8.25% for 1983 and 10% for 1984.

(ii) Where taxable income exceeds 685,200F and the "family part" system therefore does not apply, tax is first computed as for Group II: from the basic tax resulting there is a deduction varying in accordance with the amount of taxable income and the number of dependent children (e.g. on taxable income between 1,504,801F and 1,962,000F and with two dependent children the deduction is 66,312F).

From 1982 a new National Investment Levy is payable on self-employed professional income at 5% of net profit exceeding certain limits. For 1983 (but not for 1982) the levy is deductible as a "special expense" (see 2(d)(i) above).

(b) Companies etc.
The standard rate of corporation tax is 40% (with reduced rates for resident companies with taxable income not exceeding 1,312,000F) plus a surcharge for the unemployment fund at 3% for 1983 and 4% for 1984.

(c) Withholding taxes (income-taxes – other taxes may be withheld)
Payments to non-resident companies:

	General rate	Rate applied under UK double taxation agreement
Dividends	15%	5% or 15%*
Interest	15%**	NIL
Royalties	12%	5%

* The lower rate to a company owning 25% or more of voting power.
** On profit-sharing bonds only.

MALTA

Malta is a small island in an important strategic position in the Mediterranean. Its long association with the United Kingdom and the Commonwealth has been weakened in recent years and certain links with the Libyan Arab Republic have been developed.

The surtax which used to be charged on the upper levels of income of individuals has been abolished, but income tax is on a progressive scale and reaches the top rate of 65% at a comparatively low level, namely on the excess of chargeable income over £M7,000.

There were at one time very attractive tax concessions, designed to attract expatriate settlers with residence permits, but the conditions attached have been made more onerous, and there is provision for a minimum income tax liability of £M1,000.

There are certain tax incentives for approved industrial developments and there are some special concessions for investment in projects which are likely to increase exports. The tourist industry has developed considerably. The standard rate of tax on companies at the relatively low rate of 32½% is an attraction to foreign companies trading in Malta.

There is no special taxation of capital gains but gains on assets acquired with a view to profit are included in taxable income. A number of double taxation agreements are operative and partial unilateral relief is given in other cases on income from Commonwealth countries. The Maltese tax laws also apply in the island of Gozo.

1 LIST OF TAXES AND LEGISLATION

Income tax is levied on the chargeable income of individuals and companies in accordance with the Income Tax Act 1948 as subsequently amended.

2 INCOME TAX – INDIVIDUALS

(a) Income charged
Residents: Income from all sources.
Non-residents: Income received in Malta.
A temporary resident for less than 6 months in the year preceding the year of assessment is not treated as resident.

(b) Year and basis of assessment
The tax year is the calendar year. Chargeable income is that of the preceding calendar year or, in the case of a business, its accounting year ending within that year.

(c) Computation of taxable income
Expenses wholly and exclusively incurred in the production of income from any source are admissible deductions. There are a number of provisions dealing with exemptions and allowable expenses, including special allowances on investment aimed at the increase of exports. Tax is calculated on the joint income of married persons. Members of ordinary partnerships are individually assessed on their shares of income.

(i) **Business or professional income:**
Basis
Net chargeable income of the preceding calendar or accounting year. Tax incentives mainly take the form of investment allowances and accelerated depreciation for expansion projects. A loss may be set off against other income of the year and any balance unrecovered may be carried forward for future recovery.
Depreciation allowances
There are initial allowances (10% on factory etc. premises and 20% on plant and machinery) and annual allowances at prescribed rates: any allowance for a passenger vehicle, unless used for public transport or hire, is limited to a

cost basis of £M3,000. Special capital allowances are provided for approved industrial development projects.

(ii) Capital gains
There are no specific provisions for the treatment of capital gains which, in general, are included in taxable income only if property was acquired for a profit-making purpose.

(iii) Special trades etc.
Special provisions apply to insurance companies, petroleum production in Malta, shipping, air transport, cable and wireless telegraphy undertakings.

(iv) Salaries, wages etc., pensions
All gains or profits from employment or former employment, including board or residence provided, are chargeable: tax is deducted at source under a PAYE system.

(v) Dividends, interest etc.
Dividends and other distributions by companies and interest paid are liable for deduction of tax at source, normally at 32.5%, subject to double taxation agreements.

(vi) Income from letting and leasing
Rents and other income from property and the net annual value of property used by the owner or occupied rent free are chargeable.

(vii) Other income
Royalties etc. received and any miscellaneous profits or gains not otherwise covered are included in chargeable income: tax is deductible at source from payments of income to non-residents.

(d) Deductions from total income

(i) General deductions
Permitted deductions include interest on borrowed capital used to produce income, losses brought forward, pension fund contributions and life assurance.

(ii) Personal and other allowances
Married and single personal allowances and allowances for children and other dependants are given.

(iii) Tax credits
Payments under the system for collecting provisional tax in advance (based on the preceding year) on income other than from employment, together with tax suffered by deduction at source, are available for credit against the final liability.

(e) Tax deducted at source
(i) Employment income   See (c) (iv) above.
(ii) Dividends, interest etc.   See (c) (v) above.
(iii) Other income   See (c) (vii) above.

3 INCOME TAX – COMPANIES ETC.

(a) Types of undertaking charged
Partnership "en commandite" or "anonyme" constituted in Malta under the Commercial Partnerships Ordinance 1962 (equivalent to limited partnership and limited company).
Body of persons similar to the above constituted outside Malta, not more than 10% controlled by residents of Malta.
Registered co-operative society.

(b) Income charged
Resident companies etc. (i.e. those whose control and management are exercised in Malta): Income from all sources.
Non-resident companies etc. (carrying on business in Malta): Income from trading in Malta and other income received in Malta.

(c) Computation of taxable income
The computation of taxable income is in accordance with the same rules as for individuals, so far as applicable.

4 DOUBLE TAXATION AGREEMENTS

Comprehensive agreements are in force between Malta and the United Kingdom and also more than 10 other countries.
Partial relief is given in respect of income tax chargeable in

countries of the Commonwealth with which there are no double taxation agreements (provided that reciprocal relief is given) at rates varying according to whether the claimant is or is not resident in Malta.

5 RATES OF TAX

The rates of tax are subject to change from year to year, but the samples shown below for 1983 give some indication of recent rates. Amounts are stated in Maltese pounds (£M).

(a) Individuals

The income tax rates for individuals in general rise, on successive slices of chargeable income and gains, on a scale from 2% on the first £M200 to 25% on £M1,401-2,000, 40% on £M3,601-4,300 and 65% on the excess over £M7,000.

Personal reliefs (not applicable to non-residents) include:

Personal allowance: married	£M1,200
single	£M710
Each child (according to age)	£M130–160
Dependent relative	£M120

Special provisions apply to expatriate settlers with residence permits, for whom the top rate of tax is 30% on the excess of chargeable income over £M2,100 but with a minimum liability of £M1,000.

(b) Companies etc.

Standard rate of tax on chargeable profits   32.5%

Special provisions apply to profits from petroleum produced in Malta, on which the rate of tax is 50%.

(c) Withholding taxes

Payments to non-resident companies:

	General rate	Rate applied under UK double taxation agreement
Dividends	*	*
Interest	32.5%	32.5%
Royalties	32.5%	NIL

* Tax deemed to be deducted at the company rate charged on the profits out of which dividends paid – not a true withholding tax.

NETHERLANDS

The Netherlands personal taxation on income is on a highly progressive scale. There is in addition a wealth tax at 0.8% on net taxable wealth, which is assessed after some exemptions, as for instance for household effects, and subject to personal allowances for residents. There is a ceiling of 80% of taxable income for the total of income and wealth taxes. Capital gains on disposal of business assets, other than some agricultural assets, are assessed with business income: for individuals, a gain on sale of a "substantial interest" in a company is taxed at a special 20% rate: gains realised by a company on disposal of tangible assets or a substantial interest in another company may be exempt if the proceeds are taken to a special reserve and reinvested within 4 years. The rate of corporation tax for companies is relatively high at 48%, but a reduction to 43% for 1984 and 40% from 1985 is under discussion.

The taxation system of the Netherlands embodies a number of special features, among which may be mentioned:
(i) Following the recommendations of a special report (the Hofstra Report) measures were originally introduced in 1978 giving relief, for individuals and companies, to counter the increases in tax payable on business income caused by inflation. This is now given by a deduction from profits of 4% on net business capital: in addition, relief is given of 4% on opening stock in trade, except where this is valued on "base stock" or LIFO methods. Non-residents and foreign companies are eligible for these reliefs on Netherlands business capital.
(ii) An elaborate system of investment premiums was also introduced in 1978, replacing the previous arrangements for investment allowance and accelerated depreciation, designed to encourage new investment in buildings (but not land), ships, aircraft, plant and machinery. Under the Law on Investment Incentives (WIR), basic premiums are at rates varying from 8% to 14%: they are set off against tax liabilities, any

excess being paid in cash, and do not reduce the base for depreciation allowances: a uniform percentage of 12.5% is proposed from 1 January 1984. Supplementary bonuses may be given for investment in measures for countering environmental pollution and for contributing to energy conservation.

(iii) A percentage allowance for expenses is deducted from employment income, normally at 4% but for foreign resident employees increased to 35% for up to 5 years.

(iv) A new scheme of personal reliefs has been introduced in 1984, which provides for a basic relief and supplements reflecting family responsibilities and the income of a spouse or partner.

1 LIST OF TAXES

(a) Taxes on income
Income tax *(Inkomstenbelasting):* on total income of individuals, collected in part by deductions at source for:
   Wages tax *(Loonbelasting)*
   Dividend tax *(Dividendbelasting)*
Corporation tax *(Vennootschapsbelasting):* on profits of companies etc.

(b) Other taxes (not further dealt with in this summary)
Lottery tax: flat rate 15% on prizes from lotteries etc. exceeding 1.000f.
Wealth tax *(Vermogenbelasting):* tax at 0.8% on taxable wealth of individuals (assets at market value less liabilities). For residents there are a number of exemptions (e.g. goodwill, household effects, pension scheme rights) and personal allowances. Non-residents are liable for tax on certain assets less liabilities in the Netherlands (e.g. business assets of a permanent establishment or property) with no personal allowances. There is a ceiling of 80% of taxable income for the total of income and wealth taxes.

2 LEGISLATION

The basic laws are:
   Income Tax Law of 16 December 1964
   Wages Tax Law of 16 December 1964
   Dividend Tax Decree of 23 December 1965
   Corporation Tax Law of 31 October 1969
   Wealth Tax Law of 16 December 1964.
The basic laws are subject to amendment and subsidiary legislation giving detailed effect.

3 INCOME TAX – INDIVIDUALS

(a) Income charged
Residents (residence being determined by place where taxpayer regularly lives): Income from all sources
Non-residents: Income from Netherlands sources.

(b) Year and basis of assessment
The tax year is the calendar year, but profits of businesses

are assessed on the basis of the accounting period ending in the tax year.

(c) Computation of taxable income

Where both members of a married couple have earned income, their earned income and pensions are separately assessed but all other taxable income of the couple is assessed on the higher-earning spouse: where only one spouse works, the whole of the joint income is assessed on that one. Members of an ordinary partnership are assessed on their individual shares of profits.

(i) Business or professional income:

Basis

Net profit of the taxpayer's accounting period from industrial, commercial, agricultural and professional activities is assessable, profits being determined in accordance with good commercial practice. Special reliefs have been introduced to counter tax increases caused by inflation – see 6(c) below. Except where a "base stock" or LIFO method of stock valuation is used, a stock relief of 4% of opening stock is allowed together with a similar 4% on most other business assets. A special deduction from 1984 is allowed to a resident self-employed person, reducing from 4,750f. on profits up to 30,000f. to 2,700f. on profits over 80,000f. Tax-free transfers to specific reserves are allowed under some circumstances. Unrecovered losses may be carried forward for 8 years or back for up to 2 years.

Depreciation allowances

Depreciation at rates determined on the basis of normal business usage and consistently applied is an allowable deduction.

(ii) Capital gains

Gains arising from business assets are assessed with business income, but some gains from agricultural assets are exempt. In general, gains on disposal of investments are not taxable except for regular speculative transactions and gains on liquidation of a company (which may be taxed at special rates) but a gain on the sale of a "substantial interest" in a company may be taxed at a special rate of 20%. A gain on a sale of a private residence is exempt.

(iii) Special trades
Special provisions apply to the taxation of extractive industries on the continental shelf.

(iv) Salaries, wages etc., pensions
Income of all kinds from employment and former employment received from Netherlands employers is assessable: a deduction for expenses is allowed in computing taxable income, normally at 4% of income with an upper limit of 800f., but by special concession foreign employees resident in the Netherlands are allowed a 35% deduction for 5 years. Tax is deducted at source (wages tax).

(v) Income from capital
Included under this heading are dividends, interest, rents (including rental value of taxpayer's dwelling) and other income or profits not derived from business or employment. The first 700f. of interest income and the first 500f. of dividend income from Netherlands companies are exempt for individual taxpayers. There is a final withholding tax on gross income from shares etc. and from certain interest of 25% (subject to double taxation agreements).

(vi) Other income
Miscellaneous income, such as royalties received by residents, may be assessable under this heading.

(d) Deductions from total income

(i) General deductions
Permitted deductions include life insurance premiums up to 15,922f. maximum, unadjusted losses brought forward and certain annuity and similar payments.

(ii) Personal and other allowances
A new scheme of personal allowances introduced in 1984 provides for a basic relief with supplements varying with family responsibilities and the income of a spouse or partner.

(iii) Tax credits

Credit is given for tax deducted at source.

(e) Tax deducted at source

(i) Wages tax

See (c) (iv) above.

(ii) Dividend tax

See (c) (v) above.

4 CORPORATION TAX – COMPANIES ETC.

(a) Types of undertaking charged

Limited companies *(naamlooze vennootschappen – abbreviation NV)*

Closed companies

Limited partnerships

Cooperative societies and other legal entities.

For ordinary partnerships, see 3.(c) above.

Investment organisations, as defined in the 1969 Corporation Tax Law, are exempt from corporation tax subject to fulfilling prescribed conditions including substantial distributions of net income.

(b) Income charged

Domestic companies etc. (established in the Netherlands): Income from all sources

Foreign companies: Income from undertakings in the Netherlands.

(c) Computation of taxable income

Basis

Tax is computed under the same general provisions as for the income tax on individuals from business etc. profits, capital gains and income from capital (see 3(c) above). However, capital gains on disposal of tangible assets are exempt if the proceeds are placed in a special reserve and reinvested within 4 years, as are certain gains on disposal of a substantial interest in another company. Dividends from companies in which a substantial interest is held are also exempt. There is a restriction on the deductibility of a supervisory director's remuneration. See 6 (c) below for special reliefs in respect of inflation. Provision is made for a number of special incentives under the Law on Investment Incentives (WIR).

5 DOUBLE TAXATION AGREEMENTS

Comprehensive agreements are in force between the Netherlands and the United Kingdom and also more than 30 other countries.

Unilateral relief for double taxation on foreign income taxable abroad is granted to individuals and companies, equivalent to the proportion of Netherlands tax on the income in question.

6 RATES OF TAX

The rates of tax are subject to change from year to year but the samples shown below for 1984 give some indication of recent rates. Amounts are stated in guilders or florins (f.).

(a) Individuals – income tax

Rates of tax on successive slices of taxable income range from 16% on the first 9,430f. to 52% on 42,743-62,187f. and 72% on the excess over 218,075f.

From 1 January 1984 the revised scale of personal allowances deductible in arriving at taxable income is:

Group I: A basic allowance of 7,662f. is given to all residents and to non-residents with Netherlands income from employment.

Additional allowances for residents only (subject to double taxation agreements) are:

	Additional allowance
Group II: Persons aged 34 or more living alone and persons living with another of age 27 or more who has income in the range 5,027-7,662f.	2,636f.
Group III: As Group II but where the partner earns no more than 5,026f.	5,538f.
Group IV: Single parents with dependent children of age 26 or less	5,538f.
and a further addition if doing outside work and having dependent children of age 15 or less	4,231f.

Married women with employment income are entitled to separate personal allowances as above.

Other allowances are given for disability and age.

Netherlands

There is a ceiling of 80% of taxable income for the total of income tax and wealth tax.

(b) *Companies etc. – corporation tax*
Basic rate 48%
Reduced rates on profits under 50,000f.

(c) *Reliefs for the effects of inflation*
Certain reliefs were originally introduced in 1978 (following the "Hofstra Report") to counter tax increases on the business income of individuals and companies caused by inflation.
The current relief allowed is a deduction from taxable profits of 4% of net business capital as computed for tax purposes. Stock valued on "base stock" or LIFO methods or on which stock relief is allowed (see 3(c)(i) above) is not included in capital for this purpose.
For foreign companies and non-resident individuals, the reliefs only apply to Netherlands net business capital.

(d) *Withholding taxes*
Payments to non-resident companies:

	General rate	Rate applied under UK double taxation agreement
Dividends	25%	5% or 15%*
Interest (profit-sharing bonds only)	25%	NIL
Royalties	NIL	NIL

* Lower rate to company owning 25% or more of voting power.

NORWAY

Individuals and companies alike are subject to Norwegian taxation on income through the medium of Communal Income Tax, State Income Tax and the Mutual Tax (formerly known as Taxes Equalisation Levy), for all of which the general principles of assessment are the same. In addition, individuals are liable to Communal and State Capital Taxes on net wealth in Norway (other than business assets) after a deduction for personal allowances, and companies are liable for the State Capital Tax.

Capital gains are mostly taxable as ordinary income, but there are modifications in respect of investments and land and buildings which have been held for some time: gains arising from a business activity are fully taxable, subject in some cases to the re-investment of sales proceeds.

In personal taxation, the Communal and Mutual Taxes are at fixed rates, but the State Income Tax is on separate, sharply progressive, scales for jointly assessed married persons, single persons and non-residents, though the top rate of tax is fairly modest: non-residents are however subject to a final withholding tax of 25% on dividends from Norwegian companies, except as provided under double taxation agreements, which have been concluded with numerous other countries. In assessing the taxable business income of both individuals and companies, only 50% of income from fixed assets abroad is included. The profits of companies assessable to the State Income Tax are computed after deducting dividend distributions made from the current year's profits and dividends received from other Norwegian companies are liable for the State tax only.

Regional tax incentives are provided in the form of capital allowances at special rates for investment in development areas and North Norway. There are also general investment incentives whereby, under prescribed conditions, appropriations to reserve for subsequent development or promotion of exports are deductible from profits. Income from the exploitation of submarine oil deposits is taxed at normal rates plus an additional tax.

Norway

1 LIST OF TAXES

(a) Individuals and companies:
Communal Income Tax *(Inntektsskatt til communene):* Municipal and county taxes
State Income Tax *(Inntektsskatt til statskassen):* national tax
Mutual Tax *(Fellesskatt):* formerly known as Taxes Equalisation Levy
Individuals only:
Seamen's Tax
Tax on Foreign Artists' Fees
Capital Gains Tax

(b) Wealth Tax (not further dealt with in this summary)
The Communal Capital Tax is levied on resident individuals, based on their net wealth, other than fixed business assets and real property outside Norway, at an annual rate between 0.4 and 1.0% fixed by the communes: non-resident individuals and companies are similarly charged on net assets in Norway, but resident companies are exempt.

The State Capital Tax, on a similar basis, applies both to individuals (on a sliding scale between 0.3 and 1.4%) and companies (at 0.6%).

Resident individuals qualify for deduction of personal allowances from wealth for the computation of both taxes, and non-resident individuals have a deduction of 100,000kr. for the State tax only.

2 LEGISLATION

The basic laws, amended and amplified by subsequent legislation, are:
Rural Taxation Law of 18 August 1911 (for Communal and State income taxes and capital taxes), now called the Law concerning tax on capital and income (Tax Law).
Taxes Equalisation Fund Law of 24 April 1964
Seamen's Tax Law of 21 March 1947
Tax on Foreign Artists' Fees Law of 5 April 1963
Capital Gains Tax Law of 10 December 1971.

3 INDIVIDUALS' TAXES

(a) Income charged

Permanent residents (i.e. those resident for over 6 months in a year): Income from all sources except, for communal tax, dividends from Norwegian companies

Temporary residents: Remuneration for work in Norway
Non-residents: Income from all sources in Norway (see also (c) (iii) below re seamen).

(b) Year and basis of assessment

The tax year is the calendar year. Chargeable income is that of the preceding calendar year, or in the case of a business, its accounting year ending within that year.

(c) Computation of taxable income

The principles for the assessment of Communal and State Income Tax and the Mutual Tax are in general the same. Advance payments of tax are collected on employment income (deducted at source) and on other income (by instalments based on the last assessment). There is a ceiling of 80% of net taxable income for the total amount of state and communal income tax and wealth tax payable by an individual. Married couples and dependants are normally assessed in the name of the husband. Members of ordinary partnerships are individually liable for tax on their shares of partnership income.

(i) Business or professional income:

Basis
Net chargeable income is that of the preceding calendar or accounting year from all the assets of the business (except that from fixed assets abroad, of which only 50% is included in the computation). Under certain circumstances, there are deductible allocations to reserves for subsequent development, purchase of business assets, research or promotion of exports.

Depreciation allowances
Approved rates of depreciation are laid down by regulations. In some cases, an additional or an initial allowance may be claimed.

(ii) Capital gains

A State tax of 50% is levied on net gains (after tax-free allowances of 2,000-4,000kr. for individuals) from sale of any shares in a company which have been held for less than 2 calendar years. Communal and State income tax is chargeable on capital gains on disposal of other assets subject to certain exemptions (e.g. securities except as above, household effects, property used as dwelling for over 10 years). Gains arising from a business activity are fully taxable, but the liability may be deferred by using the proceeds of disposal to reduce the cost price of a similar asset or, alternatively, by allocating the proceeds to a re-investment fund or (in the case of plant, vehicles etc.) by re-investment within a year.

(iii) Special trades etc.:

Seamen

Seamen's tax (after personal, expenses and other allowances) is deducted at source from the remuneration of seamen employed in certain types of Norwegian ships in place of Communal and State income tax.

Submarine oil deposits

Income from the exploitation of oil deposits is taxed under separate regulations (law of 13 June 1975) at the normal rates plus a special additional State tax at a rate fixed annually – currently 25% on income exceeding 10% of operating costs.

Foreign artists

A flat-rate tax (without any deduction for expenses) is deducted at source from fees earned in Norway by foreign entertainers, artists, musicians and athletes, subject to certain exemptions. The tax (at 20% for artists engaged by others and 10% for those making their own arrangements) replaces normal taxation.

(iv) Salaries, wages etc., pensions

All forms of income from employment or former employment are assessable, after regulated deductions for contributions and other expenses: in most cases tax is deducted at source.

(v) Dividends, interest etc.

Dividends and other distributions by companies and interest are assessable, subject to an initial exemption of 2,000kr. for single persons and 4,000kr. for persons with dependants: dividends from Norwegian companies are liable for State but not Communal tax: final withholding tax at 25% is deducted from dividends paid by Norwegian companies to non-resident shareholders, subject to the terms of double taxation agreements.

(vi) Income from letting and leasing

Rents received are assessable, including a notional amount for an owner-occupied dwelling house: only 50% of income from property abroad is assessed.

(vii) Other income

Royalties and miscellaneous income or gains not otherwise covered are included in taxable income.

(d) Deductions from total income

(i) General deductions

Permitted deductions include limited amounts for insurance, pension contributions and interest paid. Losses may be set off against other income of the year and any amounts not so adjusted may be carried forward in most cases for up to 10 years: losses are not transferable on change of ownership of a business.

(ii) Personal and other allowances

Allowances given include married and single personal allowances for communal tax, a deduction from earned income varying with the number of dependent children, and allowances for age or disability: a tax-exempt allowance is paid by the State for children under 17 and a deduction from tax is allowed for older children.

(iii) Tax credits

Credit is given in the final assessment for advance payments of tax (see (c) above) and for tax deducted at source.

(e) Tax deducted at source
  (i) Employment income: See (c) (iii) (seamen) and (iv) above.
  (ii) Dividends, interest etc.: See (c) (v) above.

4 COMPANIES' ETC. TAXES

(a) Types of undertaking charged
Joint-stock companies *(Aksjeselskaper)*
Limited partnerships
Ordinary partnerships *(Kompaniskaper)* – individual partners taxed on their share of profits
Other associations (e.g. co-operatives, building societies)

(b) Income charged
Resident companies etc. (i.e. those whose head offices or seats of management are in Norway): Income from all sources
Non-resident companies etc.: Income from all sources in Norway.

(c) Computation of taxable income
The computation of taxable income is in the main in accordance with the same rules as for individuals, capital gains being, in general, treated as ordinary income. Companies etc. taxed as separate entities are liable for Communal and State income tax and the mutual tax: advance payments of tax are not required. Dividends from other Norwegian companies are subject to State income tax only. Dividend distributions from the current year's profits, when made in accordance with Norwegian law (which requires *inter alia* allocations to a reserve fund) are allowable deductions in calculating profits for the purpose of State income tax. There is no over-riding limit on total tax of the kind which applies to individuals.

5 DOUBLE TAXATION AGREEMENTS

Comprehensive agreements are in force between Norway and the United Kingdom and also over 40 other countries: in addition, agreements with the UK have been extended to include 25 other territories of, or formerly of, the Commonwealth.
  Unilateral relief is granted to Norwegian residents on income from personal work carried out abroad on which tax has been paid abroad.

6 RATES OF TAX

The rates of tax are subject to change from year to year, but the sample figures shown below for income of the year 1983 give an indication of recent rates. Amounts are stated in Kroner (kr.).

(a) Individuals

(i) Communal income tax and mutual tax

The Communal income tax is fixed at 21% and the mutual tax, computed on the same basis, is at 2%, making a total of 23%.

The local taxes are not deductible in arriving at profits for State income tax.

(ii) State income tax

Rates vary on successive slices of taxable income and in accordance with the class of taxpayer:

Class 1: resident single persons (or married persons assessed separately) and non-residents.

Class 2: resident married persons assessed jointly and single persons with dependent children.

The personal allowance given in arriving at taxable income is:

Resident single persons	42,000kr.
Resident married persons	78,000kt.
Non-residents	1,500kr.

Samples of the rates are:

Class	1	2
4% on first	38,000kr.	26,000kr.
9% on	38,001 – 53,000kr.	26,001 – 42,000kr.
26% on	75,001 – 97,000kr.	64,001 – 86,000kr.
41% on over	222,000kr.	212,000kr.

Tax on dividends to non-residents is in general at 25%.

Allowances in the form of tax credits are given for children, the amounts being dependent on the marital status of the taxpayer and the ages and incomes of the children. There are also earned income deductions for taxpayers with minor children.

(iii) Personal etc. allowances to residents for communal tax
include:

Personal allowance:	Class 1	11,300kr.
	Class 2	22,600kr.

(b) Companies etc.

(i) Communal income tax and mutual tax:
Rates are as for individuals, total 23%.

(ii) State income tax:
Standard rate on taxable income is 27.8%.
Special rates apply to e.g. building societies,
co-operatives, savings banks.

(c) Withholding taxes
Payments to non-resident companies:

	General rate	Rate applied under UK double taxation agreement
Dividends	25%	10% or 15%*
Interest	NIL	NIL
Royalties	NIL	NIL

* Lower rate to company owning 10% or more of voting
power.

PORTUGAL

The tax legislation of Portugal distinguishes between (a) metropolitan Portugal and the adjacent islands (i.e. the Azores and Madeira), referred to herein simply as "Portugal", and (b) other Portuguese territories overseas. Only "Portugal" is dealt with in this summary.

There is a schedular system of taxation and income assessed under the separate schedular taxes (e.g. professional tax or industrial tax), less the amount of tax so assessed, is subject to a surtax known as the complementary tax which applies both to companies and to individuals on differing scales. For the purpose of the industrial tax, taxpayers are divided into three groups: those in Group A, which includes most taxpayers other than those in a small way of business, are assessed on the basis of their accounting profits: those in Groups B and C are assessed on an arbitrarily assumed income and are not therefore dealt with in this summary.

In personal taxation, the combined effect of the schedular taxes, surcharges and the complementary tax is to produce highly progressive rates of tax. There are at present (possibly temporary) surcharges on the industrial tax, capital gains tax, tax on income from capital and property tax. Tax incentives are available for concerns promoting new industrial developments.

There is a comprehensive system of withholding taxes, the effective rates for these on payments to some countries outside Portugal being dependent on the provisions of double taxation agreements, of which a number are in existence.

Portugal

1 LIST OF TAXES

There is a schedular system of taxation, the principal taxes being:

(a) Schedular taxes
(i) Professional tax *(imposto profissional):* levied on the earned income of individuals from employment or professional activities.
(ii) Industrial tax *(contribuicão industrial):* levied on the net profits of commercial or industrial activities of companies and self-employed persons.
(iii) Tax on income from capital *(imposto de capitais):* a withholding tax deducted at source from dividends, interest, royalties etc.
(iv) Property tax: levied on the rental or rateable value of property.

(b) Other taxes
(i) Complementary tax *(imposto complementar):* an additional tax, levied (after deduction of schedular taxes) on all income of individuals and on retained profits of resident companies.
(ii) Capital gains tax *(imposto de mais valias):* levied on gains on disposal of business assets and in certain other cases.
(iii) Payroll taxes, for social welfare and unemployment benefits, at rates totalling approximately 10½% on earnings, are payable by employees. (Not further dealt with in this summary.)

2 INDIVIDUALS' TAXATION

(a) Income charged

(i) **For professional tax:**
Income from earnings arising in Portugal

(ii) **For complementary tax:**
Residents: Income from all sources
Non-residents: Income received in Portugal

(b) Year and basis of assessment
The tax year is the calendar year, and taxes are assessed on the income of the preceding year.

(c) Computation of taxable income

Tax is separately assessed under each of the schedular headings and the total of the income so assessed, reduced by any admissible exemptions, allowances or deductions, is included in the assessment for complementary tax: the amounts of the schedular taxes are included in the deductions in computing taxable income for complementary tax. Married persons are jointly assessed. Partnerships, a form of association not very frequently used, are assessed as separate entities.

(i) Business or professional income:

Basis

Income from self-employed commercial or industrial activities, after any admissible exemptions or deductions, e.g. for necessary expenses incurred in acquisition of the income, is assessable for industrial tax. Certain special tax exemptions or reductions are available as incentives to promote industrial development, e.g. in setting up new installations or manufacturing processes. Unrelieved losses may be carried forward for up to 5 years.

Professional income earned by lawyers, doctors, engineers, artists etc. is assessable for professional tax: taxpayers with a permanent place of business are assessed on net income after deduction of necessary expenses, but in other cases there are no admissible deductions from gross income.

Depreciation allowances

Reasonable straight-line rates of depreciation are allowed subject to agreement with the revenue authorities.

(ii) Capital gains

Capital gains tax is payable:
1. on sale of professional premises or other capital assets of a business or profession at 12%,
2. on the sale of urban land for development at 24%.

There is a surcharge of 15% for 1983 and 1984. Industrial tax and complementary tax are payable on gains on disposal of building land bought for re-sale or disposed of within 2 years of purchase.

Portugal

(iii) Special trades

Self-employed income from farming is included in the income assessed for complementary tax. There is provision for a schedular tax on agriculture but the application of this has been suspended.

(iv) Salaries, wages etc., pensions

Income from employment, including expense allowances exceeding prescribed limits and bonuses is assessable for professional tax: retirement pensions are exempt. Tax is deductible at source, the amount so suffered being adjusted on the basis of the annual return of income.

(v) Dividends, interest etc.

Tax on income from capital is withheld at source from dividends and other distributions made by companies, and from interest, as a final withholding tax.

(vi) Income from letting and leasing

Rents received or the annual rateable value of property, after prescribed allowances for maintenance etc., are liable for property tax at rates varying with the type of property (14-18% plus surcharges): an owner-occupier is taxed on the rateable value. The taxable income, less property tax, is included in income on which complementary tax is assessed.

(vii) Other income

Income from royalties etc. is subject to tax on income from capital withheld at source, and the net amount after tax is included in income for complementary tax purposes.

(d) *Deductions from total income* (for complementary tax purposes)

(i) General deductions

Admissible deductions include schedular taxes paid and life or accident insurance premiums up to a specified limit.

(ii) Personal and other allowances

Married and single personal allowances and allowances for children and for earned income are given. A fixed total relief of Esc.80,000 is prescribed for non-residents.

(e) **Tax deducted at source**

   (i) Employment income   See (c) (iv) above.

   (ii) Dividends, interest etc.   See (c) (v) above.

   (iii) Royalties etc.   See (c) (vii) above.

3 COMPANIES' TAXATION

(a) **Types of undertaking charged**
Portuguese companies:
(i) "SARL" *(Sociedade anónima de responsabilidade limitada)* with at least 10 share holders: the shares are freely transferable.
(ii) "Limitada" or "Quota company" *(Sociedade por quotas)* with at least 2 "quota-holders": quotas, which may not take the form of shares, are transferable by deed.
Branches of foreign companies.

(b) **Income charged**
Portuguese companies and branches of foreign companies are assessed for industrial tax on commercial or industrial profits derived from Portugal or received there from foreign sources: complementary tax is based on the industrial tax assessment.

(c) **Computation of taxable income**
The computation of taxable income is based on the accounting profit for the preceding year or accounting period ending in that year, less any exemptions and after making any adjustments required for tax purposes. Dividends or interest received from Portuguese companies are exempt if more than 25% of the share capital has been held by the investing company for two years or more. Any tax suffered by deduction at source from dividend and interest income and property tax paid in the year are deductible in arriving at the industrial tax assessment. Reasonable straight-line rates of depreciation of fixed assets are accepted. The income assessable for complementary tax is reduced by industrial tax paid in the year and also by dividend distributions declared.

    A branch of a foreign company is not liable for complementary tax if control of the branch is not exercised in Portugal, nor are branch profits which are remitted abroad subject to withholding tax on income from capital.

Capital gains tax is assessable as at 2.(c) (ii) above, but profits and capital gains re-invested within 3 years may be deductible from taxable profits.

4 DOUBLE TAXATION

Comprehensive double taxation agreements are in force between Portugal and the United Kingdom and also about 10 other countries.

5 RATES OF TAX

Rates of tax are subject to change from year to year but the sample figures shown below for 1983 give an indication of recent rates. Amounts are stated in escudos (Esc.).

(a) *Professional tax* is on a progressive scale, on the whole of taxable income (i.e. not on successive slices), rising from 2% where taxable income is between Esc.202,801 and 250,000, to 10% where it is between Esc.450,001 and 600,000 and 22% where it exceeds Esc.1,350,000.

(b) *Industrial tax* is at a basic rate of 30% on the first Esc.3,000,000 taxable profit and 40% thereafter. There is in addition a local surcharge of up to 10% and an extraordinary addition for 1983 and possibly 1984 of 10%.

(c) *Complementary tax*

(i) **Individuals:**

the rate on successive slices of taxable income rises on a scale from 4% married on the first Esc.220,000 (4.8% single on the first Esc.180,000) to 26% married on Esc.1,300,001 – 1,580,000 (31.2% single on Esc.1,080,001-1,320,000) and 70% married on the excess over Esc.2,740,000 (80% single on excess over Esc.2,280,000).

Personal reliefs for resident individuals include:

Personal allowance	married Esc.180,000
	single Esc.120,000
Children	Esc.25,000–40,000 per child
	according to age
Earned income	30% (maximum Esc.50,000)

There is a general allowance of Esc.80,000 for a non-resident.

(ii) Companies (resident)
The rate rises in stages from 6% on the first Esc.120,000
to 12% on the excess over Esc.6,000,000.

(d) Withholding taxes
Payments to non-resident companies:

	*General rate***	*Rate under UK double taxation agreement*
Dividends	15%	10% or 15%*
Interest: bond interest	12%	10%
deposit interest	18%	10%
other taxable interest	30%	10%
Royalties	15%	5%

  * The lower rate for payments to UK companies with 25%
voting power.
** The rates are currently subject to a 10% surcharge.

ROMANIA

The approach to taxation in the Socialist Republic of Romania is, as might be expected, somewhat different from that in a more open economy. There are provisions dealing with trades and businesses carried on independently – i.e. by individuals and associations other than State enterprises – and there are several separate taxable categories of income from professional work. Income from employment is subject to a final withholding tax deducted by the employer, the rate for an employee with more than three dependants being reduced by 30%.

The taxation provisions most likely to be relevant to foreigners are:

1. Detailed regulations for the taxation of different kinds of agency of foreign commercial firms, which is assessed either on income less expenses or, under some circumstances, on a scale based on the value of contracts signed or the number of employees.
2. Final withholding taxes deducted from payments of income to non-residents such as performance fees, income from air and sea transport, certain interest, commission, consultancy fees and royalties.

Romanian law provides for the formation of "joint companies", with foreign participation of up to 49%, intended to contribute to the development of the economy. These are taxed at a fixed standard rate on income less approved expenses (including depreciation), with an additional tax on profits remitted abroad and a reduction for profits re-invested. Such companies are guaranteed the right to transfer abroad the shares of profit due to foreign participants.

1 LIST OF TAXES AND LEGISLATION

The basic legislation governing the income taxes in force in the
Socialist Republic of Romania consists of the laws referred to
below.

(i) **Income tax:**
   levied on the income of individuals and corporate bodies,
   other than State enterprises (Decree No. 153 of 1954).

(ii) **Withholding tax:**
   levied on certain income of non-resident individuals and
   companies (Decree No. 276 of 1973).

(iii) **Tax on joint companies:**
   levied on the profits of joint companies formed in
   Romania (Decree No. 425 of 1972).

2 INDIVIDUALS' TAXATION

Much of the material relating to individuals also applies to
corporate bodies, but further provisions concerning "joint companies" formed in Romania are referred to at 3. below.

(a) Income charged
   Both residents and non-residents are chargeable to income
   tax on income from all sources received in or derived from
   Romania. Where the distinction is relevant (e.g. under the
   provisions for withholding tax), an individual who stays not
   more than 120 days in a year in Romania is treated as
   non-resident.

(b) Year and basis of assessment
   The income year for tax purposes is the calendar year.
   Quarterly advance payments of tax, based on the income of
   the previous year, are normally required.

(c) Computation of taxable income
   Taxable income is assessed for income tax under six different
   categories, dealt with below, which are subject to differing
   provisions and rates of tax. There are no personal allowances
   as such, but for childless persons the standard rates of tax are
   increased.

Romania

(i) Business or professional income
Basis
Four separate income categories come under this heading:

1. Income from independent personal services, trade, and enterprises other than State units. This includes the income of professional persons working independently and all kinds of trade carried on by individuals and companies. Taxable income consists of aggregate receipts less expenses incurred in producing the income. There is no provision for carrying forward losses.
   Agencies of foreign commercial firms, authorised to operate in Romania, are taxable under this category. Rates of tax vary according to the type of agency:

   a. For an agency paid by its firm on a commission basis or which earns profits from its own activities, tax is payable at graduated rates on taxable income (gross income less expenses incurred in producing it): there is however a minimum standard taxable income, based on the number of employees.
   b. For an agency not entitled to a commission but authorised to sign contracts for its firm, the taxable income is calculated on a sliding scale based on the value of contracts signed.
   c. For an agency not entitled to a commission and not earning income on its own account, taxable income is assessed as a lump sum depending on the number of employees.

2. Contributions to newspapers and other publications and the income of physicians from paid consultations: tax is on a sliding scale based on monthly income. A final withholding tax is deducted at source.
3. Income of actors, musicians etc.: tax is on a sliding scale based on monthly income. Tax, normally at 25%, is deducted from payments to non-residents.
4. Income from artistic, literary and scientific work. Expenses at fixed rates are deducted in arriving at taxable income. A final witholding tax is deducted at source: tax, normally at 25%, is deducted from payments to non-residents.

(ii) Capital gains

Capital gains do not appear to be specifically referred to in the Romanian tax decrees: provisions relating to their taxation are however included in the double taxation agreement with the United Kingdom.

(iii) Special trades

For craftsmen working independently in certain trades, net annual taxable income is officially laid down and is dealt with under the category of (i) 1. above.

There are provisions relating to withholding tax, normally at 15%, on the income of non-residents from air and sea transport.

(iv) Salaries, wages etc., pensions

Final withholding tax is deducted by the employer from income from employment. The tax is reduced by 30% if the employee has more than three dependants without separate income.

(v) Dividends, interest etc.

Income of this sort is not specifically referred to in the Romanian tax decrees, except that interest on commercial credits paid to a non-resident is subject to a withholding tax, normally at 15%.

(vi) Income from letting and leasing

Gross income less expenses (on a fixed scale for the rent of furnished rooms) is taxable as a separate category.

(vii) Other income

Provision is made for deduction of withholding tax, normally at 15%, from payments to non-residents such as commission and consultancy fees, at 20% from royalties etc. and at 25% from "cultural royalties" (e.g. on entertainment rights).

(d) Deductions from total income

(i) General deductions

Any deductions permitted are made from the individual categories of income.

(ii) Personal and other allowances

There are no separate personal allowances but, subject to certain exemptions, income under all categories of persons aged 25 or over who are childless is subject to income tax increased by 10% for incomes up to 24,000 lei per annum and by 20% on higher incomes.

(iii) Tax credits
No credit arises from the withholding taxes since these are final taxes on the respective categories of income from which they are deducted.

(e) Tax deducted at source
The rates of tax specified as deductible from payments to non-residents are the minimum rates which may be increased if the country of the non-resident taxes similar payments to Romanians at higher rates.

(i) Income from literary, artistic etc. work and fees: See (c) (i) 2. and 4. above.

(ii) Income from employment: See (c) (iv) above.

(iii) Income payments to non-residents: See (c) (i) 3. and 4., (c) (iii), (c) (v) and (c) (vii) above.

3 COMPANIES' TAXATION

(a) Types of undertaking charged
Joint Companies formed under Romanian law (in which foreign participation of up to 49% is allowed)
Other corporate bodies (other than State enterprises)

(b) Income charged
Both resident and non-resident corporate bodies are chargeable to tax on income from all sources received in Romania. A non-resident company (e.g. for the purpose of the withholding tax provisions) is one whose registered office is outside Romania.

(c) Computation of taxable income
Joint companies formed under Romanian law are taxed on taxable income, namely gross income less expenses including depreciation and certain transfers to reserve: a further tax is charged on any profits transferred abroad. Other corporate bodies are taxed in accordance with the same rules as individuals, so far as applicable.

4 DOUBLE TAXATION

Comprehensive double taxation agreements are in force between Romania and the United Kingdom and about 20 other countries.

5 RATES OF TAX

Rates of tax are subject to change from year to year, but the sample figures shown below which were operative for 1981 (and apparently still applied in 1983) give an indication of recent rates. Amounts are stated in Romanian lei.

(a) Individuals and corporate bodies (other than "Joint Companies")

There are separate graduated scales of tax for each category of taxable income. Samples of the rates are:

		Initial exemption	Tax on annual income of		
			12000	*24000*	*100000 lei*
(i)	Salaries etc. ((c) (iv))	lei 10932	600	3120	18720
(ii)	Literary contributions etc.				
	((c) (i) 2.)	–	1284	3768	22524
(iii)	Artistic etc. work ((c) (i) 4.)	–	1140	3432	20724
(iv)	Independent services etc.				
	((c) (i) 1.)	–	2740	6790	38390
(v)	Rents etc. ((c) (vi))	–	4301	10061	68881

There is a maximum average rate of 45% for individuals on income as above except rents etc. For companies, there is a maximum average rate of 60% for income under headings (iii) and (iv) above. See 2.(d) (ii) above about increases for childless taxpayers.

(b) Joint Companies

Standard rate on taxable profits	30%
Reduced rate on profits re-invested for a committed period of 5 years or more	24%
Additional tax on profits remitted abroad	10%

(c) Withholding taxes

Payments to non-resident companies:

	General rate	Rate applied under UK double taxation agreement
Interest	15%	10%
Royalties	20%	15%

See also 2. (e) (iii) above.

SPAIN

In 1979 major changes were made in the Spanish tax system, which applies to Spanish mainland territory, the Balearic and Canary Islands and the North African ports of Ceuta and Melilla. Before these changes, a "schedular" system was used under which tax was collected from individuals and companies at various fixed rates divided over a number of separate schedules (e.g. land tax, industrial tax, income from personal work): the tax so charged was treated as being on account of the taxpayer's liability for the general income tax, at progressive rates on individuals, or the company tax for companies. The schedular taxes have now been either abolished or absorbed into the system of local taxes which are charged in addition to the national taxes on income. The local taxes are at various rates fixed locally and were formerly either separate local taxes or surcharges on types of income chargeable to schedular taxes.

Personal taxation is on a progressive scale which is not particularly steep, considering the high level of taxable income at which the top rates come into operation: there is also a wealth tax (the top rate for which is also on a very high level of wealth) in addition to the local taxes. Tax is withheld at source from most payments to non-residents.

A number of tax incentives are given in the form of tax credits, which are based on the amount of the taxpayer's expenditure for purposes such as investments in new plant, research and development, creation of new jobs and investments in certain approved publicly quoted securities.

1 LIST OF TAXES AND LEGISLATION

Following the reorganisation of the tax system in 1978, by the income tax laws quoted below, taxes levied from 1 January 1979 are:

(a) Income tax levied on individuals *(Impuesto sobre la Renta de las Personas Fisicas)* under Law 44/1978.

(b) Company tax levied on companies and all other legal entities not taxed as individuals *(Impuesto sobre Sociedades)* under Law 61/1978.

(c) The following are not further dealt with in this summary:

(i) Local taxes:
These take a number of different forms and are payable by individuals and companies at varying rates fixed locally by municipalities or provinces, subject to specified maximum rates. The taxes comprise urban and agricultural land taxes (based on rated value), an industrial tax and tax on income from personal work (licence fees). Local taxes paid are deductible expenses for income tax purposes.

(ii) Wealth tax:
Levied on the net wealth of resident individuals and on the net wealth in Spain of non-residents: exemptions are allowed to residents, for a married taxpayer 9 million ptas. and for a single taxpayer 6 million ptas., increased for children and dependants: the tax is on a sliding scale on successive slices of taxable wealth rising from 0.2% to 2% on the excess over 2,500 million ptas.

2 INDIVIDUALS' INCOME TAX

(a) Income charged
Residents: Income from all sources.
Non-residents: Income obtained in Spain or paid by a Spanish resident.

(b) Year and basis of assessment
The tax year is the calendar year or, in the case of a business etc., its accounting year ending in that year. Individuals are

required to make payments on account, based on 60% of the
liability for the previous year.

(c) Computation of taxable income

Total income, subject to exemptions, after admissible
deductions and set-off of losses, is chargeable. In certain
circumstances, evidence of living standards suggesting an
income higher than that included in the return of income
may be used as the basis for a revised assessment. Married
persons are jointly assessed. Members of associations of
persons which have no independent legal identity are taxed
as individuals, provided the members are separately responsible for their shares of any tax liability. There are a number
of special incentives encouraging new investments by
individuals.

(i) Business or professional income:

Basis
Net income after deducting necessary expenses is
assessable.
Depreciation allowances
Genuine amounts for depreciation written off in the
accounts are allowable, subject to specified maximum
permissible rates.

(ii) Capital gains

Income tax is payable on gains on disposal of movable
and real property: exemptions include gains on disposal
of business assets or an owner-occupied dwelling if the
proceeds are reinvested in similar assets, and there is
some relief for other assets which have been held for
more than a year.

(iii) Special trades

Special provisions apply to shipping and air transport
and the exploitation of hydrocarbon deposits.

(iv) Salaries, wages etc., pensions

Income from employment is subject to deduction of tax
at source. Pensions paid by approved pension schemes
are exempt from tax.

(v) Dividends, interest etc.
Tax is deducted at source from payments to non-residents of dividends and interest. A partial imputation tax system has been applied since 1979 to dividends received by residents.

(vi) Income from letting and leasing
Rents received and a notional amount on an owner-occupied property are assessable. Withholding tax is deducted from payments to non-residents.

(vii) Other income
Miscellaneous taxable income includes royalties and fees: withholding tax is deductible from payments to non-residents.

(d) Deductions from total income

(i) General deductions
Life assurance premiums and any losses not recovered from specific sources of income are deductible: unrelieved income and capital losses may be carried forward for up to 5 years for recovery from taxable income or gains.

(ii) Personal and other allowances
Personal reliefs, given to residents by means of tax credits, include a general relief, earned income allowance and reliefs for a spouse and children or other dependants.

(iii) Tax credits
Credits are allowed for tax suffered by deduction at source, for personal reliefs and for double taxation where applicable.

(e) Tax deducted at source
(i) Employment income   See (c) (iv) above.
(ii) Dividends, interest etc.   See (c) (v) above.
(iii)Rents etc.   See (c) (vi) above.
(iv)Royalties, fees etc.   See (c) (vii) above.

3   COMPANY TAX

(a) Types of undertaking charged
All types of company and partnership except associations of the type referred to in 2.(c) above whose members are taxable as individuals.

(b) Income charged
Resident companies (i.e. those incorporated under Spanish law and others whose registered office *(domicilio social)* or place of effective management is on Spanish territory): Income from all sources
Non-resident companies: Income derived from Spain, including capital gains on assets situated in Spain.

(c) Computation of taxable income
Income of all kinds less necessary expenses and depreciation (normally as shown in the accounts) is assessable. Capital gains on disposal of business assets are exempt if the proceeds are re-invested in similar assets within a limited period. Inter-company dividends are 50% exempted from company tax – or 100% where a 25% interest is held in the paying company. Certain tax incentives and reliefs are granted to industries of "preferential interest" to the economy, for investments in development areas and in a number of other cases.

4   DOUBLE TAXATION

There are double taxation agreements in force between Spain and the United Kingdom and also more than 15 other countries. Unilateral relief is given in respect of income arising in a country with which Spain has no such agreement, either for the foreign tax or the Spanish tax which would have been payable on the income had it arisen in Spain, whichever is less.

5   RATES OF TAX

The rates of tax are subject to variation from year to year, but the samples shown below for 1984 give an indication of recent rates. Amounts are stated in pesetas (ptas.).

(a) Individuals

Income tax is levied on a graduated scale for successive slices of taxable income, rising from 16.11% on the first 200,000 ptas. to 20.46% on 800,001 – 1,000,000 ptas., 39.36% on 4,200,001 – 4,600,000 ptas. and 66% on the excess over 12,200,000 ptas. There is an overall limit on the income tax of residents of 46% of taxable income or 70% for income tax and wealth tax combined.

Personal reliefs for residents, given as tax credits, include:

General personal tax credit   17,000 ptas.
    (increased by 50% each if more than one member of the family unit has earned income exceeding 150,000ptas. per annum)

Spouse		18,000ptas.
Child – first 3	each	14,000ptas.
others	each	19,000ptas.
Earned income	1% (maximum	10,000ptas.)

(b) Companies

Standard rate of company tax 35%.

(c) Withholding taxes

Payments to non-resident companies:

	General rate	*Rate applied under UK double taxation agreement*
Dividends	16%	10% or 15%*
Interest	16%	12%
Royalties	16%	10%

*The lower rate to a company owning 10% or more of voting power.

In the 1984 Budget, the general rate of withholding tax on income from moveable capital is being increased to 18%.

SWEDEN

Sweden has a system of taxation of income based on a uniform national income tax and local taxes varying within fairly narrow limits in the different municipalities. In addition, there is a national net worth tax or wealth tax. There is no separate capital gains tax, but most kinds of short-term capital gain are taxable as ordinary income and the liability is scaled down after longer periods of ownership. Tax incentives are provided by a system of tax-free investment and profit equalisation reserves and special allowances for research and development costs.

Personal taxation is on a highly progressive scale and, though the basic top rate has been reduced, a supplementary tax is now levied on the higher levels of income. There is however a ceiling of 80% for the marginal top rate of national and local income taxes on income up to 219,000Kr and 84% above this. Non-residents do not qualify for the allowances and exemptions given to residents, but a special reduced rate of local income tax (10%) is applied to them.

The standard rate of national income tax on companies has been reduced, but there is now a temporary tax on dividend distributions of Swedish companies and possible plans for compulsory profit-sharing levies are under consideration.

Sweden has an unusually large number of double taxation agreements with other countries, and a form of unilateral relief is available where no tax treaty exists. There is no withholding tax on interest or royalties and on dividends tax is withheld only from payments to non-residents.

1 LIST OF TAXES

(a) National Income Tax:
Levied on the income or profits of individuals and companies.

(b) The following taxes are not further dealt with in this summary:

(i) *National Annual Net Worth Tax:*
a wealth tax levied on the total net worth of individuals and non-resident companies, subject to the effect of double taxation agreements. The tax is charged on a graduated scale: after exemption for the first 300,000Kr, the rate rises from 1% to 4% on net worth over 1,800,000Kr. Non-resident individuals are liable for the tax on certain assets in Sweden and non-resident companies are liable on their investment in Sweden. A mini-Budget in 1983 proposed an increase of 10% in the rate for 1984.

(ii) *Local Income Tax:*
levied on the income or profits of individuals and companies at varying flat rates for the different local authority districts, generally about 30%: the Stockholm rate for 1984, excluding Church tax, is 29.2%. For resident individuals there is a personal allowance of 7,500Kr. Non-resident individuals and companies are charged at a special rate of 10% on income which is not attributable to any particular local authority. Local income tax paid is deductible by companies, but not by individuals, in computing national income tax.

2 INDIVIDUALS' INCOME TAX

(a) Income charged
Residents: Income from all sources
Non-residents: Income derived from Sweden

(b) Year and basis of assessment
The tax year is the calendar year and individuals are assessed on this basis.

(c) Computation of taxable income
Expenses incurred in the acquisition of income are in general admissible deductions in arriving at taxable income. Married

persons are separately assessed on their earned incomes ("A" Income) and the spouse with the higher earned income is assessed on their joint investment income ("B" Income). Members of partnerships are individually liable for tax on their shares of profit and capital.

(i) **Business or professional income:**
Basis
Normal business expenses are admissible deductions in arriving at taxable profits. Stock in trade may not be written down to a valuation below a certain percentage of cost.

Depreciation allowances
Allowances are given for depreciation of buildings on a straight line basis at rates dependent on the life of the assets. For plant and machinery depreciation allowed is normally up to 30% on the declining balance, but straight line depreciation of 20% is permitted if this results in a larger allowance in any year. There are provisions for accelerated depreciation (not at present being applied) and investment allowances in certain cases.

(ii) **Capital gains**
There is no separate capital gains tax but taxable gains are subject to national and local income taxes.
Land and buildings: costs used to calculate the gain are adjusted by an index reflecting price rises but, under new rules applicable from 1984, this only applies after 3 years' ownership.
Shares etc.: the whole gain on realisation of shares held for less than two years is taxable and 40% of the gain in other cases.
Other property: the whole gain on realisation of assets held for less than two years is taxable and a reducing percentage of the gain is taxable after longer ownership, with exemption after 5 years.

A gain on disposal of machinery used in a business is taxed as business profit and not as a capital gain. Capital losses may be carried forward and offset against capital gains in the next 6 years.

(iii) Special trades
There are special tax incentives for oil companies and large users of oil products.

(iv) Salaries, wages etc., pensions
Expenses incurred in acquiring the income (minimum allowance 1,000Kr) are an admissible deduction in arriving at taxable income.

There is a system of deduction of tax at source from all income from employment or former employment ("A" Income).

(v) Dividends, interest, etc.
A 30% final withholding tax, sometimes called "the coupon tax", is deducted from dividends from resident companies to non-residents, subject to the effect of double taxation agreements. Tax is not deducted from interest payments or from dividends to residents.

(vi) Income from letting and leasing
There is a system of attributing imputed rental income from residential property, including the owner's residence, based on the assessed value.

(vii) Other income
No tax is withheld at source from payments of royalty income.

(d) Deductions from total income

(i) General deductions
Life and accident insurance premiums and pension scheme contributions are admissible within specified limits. Losses on one category of income may be set off against other income, and any amounts unrelieved may be carried forward for up to 10 years.

(ii) Personal and other allowances
There is no general personal allowance but there is an initial tax exemption range in the tax scale, and there are allowances for care of children and in case of age or infirmity. There is no tax exemption for dependent children but tax-free family allowances are paid.

(iii) Tax credits
Credit is given for tax suffered by deduction at source and for relief under double taxation agreements.

(c) Tax deducted at source
(i) Employment income   See (c) (iv) above.
(ii) Dividends, interest etc.   See (c) (v) above.

3 COMPANIES' INCOME TAX

(a) Types of undertaking charged
Companies and other associations (but not partnerships).

(b) Income charged
Resident companies etc. (i.e. those registered in Sweden or whose central management or principal business is in Sweden): Income from all sources
Non-resident companies etc.: Income from real property, business or capital gains derived from a permanent establishment in Sweden

(c) Computation of taxable income
Companies are assessed on the basis of their most recent accounting period ending prior to March 1st in the tax year (calendar year). The computation of taxable profit is in general in accordance with the same rules as for individuals, so far as applicable. Dividends from a company in which a 25% interest is held are exempt. In some cases, dividends paid on newly issued shares may be deductible in arriving at taxable income. Realised capital gains are liable for normal rates of national and local income taxes. A company carrying on a business is permitted to allocate 50% of pre-tax profits to a tax-free reserve for future investment in fixed assets, or for such purposes as research and development, but 50% of the allocation must be deposited in a blocked interest-free account with the National Bank. Amounts are released with Government approval. Allocations may also be made to a profit equalisation reserve, subject to special conditions. Local income taxes and indirect taxes are permissible deductions in the computation of profits of companies for national income tax.

4 DOUBLE TAXATION

Comprehensive double taxation agreements are in force between Sweden and the United Kingdom and also over 40 other countries: in addition, the UK agreement has been extended to a number of formerly dependent territories. Unilateral relief is granted for foreign tax not covered by a double taxation agreement.

5 RATES OF TAX

The rates of tax are subject to change from year to year, but the sample figures shown below for the year 1984 give an indication of recent rates. Amounts are stated in Swedish kroner (Kr).

(a) Individuals

Basic rates of national income tax rise on a graduated scale on successive slices of taxable income, ranging, after an initial exemption of 7,600Kr, from 3% on the next 22,800Kr to 17% on 68,401 – 76,000Kr and 32% on the excess over 228,000Kr. Supplementary income tax is also levied on taxable income over 121,600Kr, starting at 3% and rising to 20% on the excess over 342,000Kr.

There are provisions applying a ceiling to the combined marginal rate of national and local income tax on the highest slices of income.

For residents, there are allowances for care of children, age and infirmity.

(b) Companies

The standard rate of national income tax for 1983 is 40%, but for accounting periods starting after 31 December 1983 the rate is 32%. For years of assessment ending after 30 June 1983 a temporary tax of 20% on dividend distributions made by Swedish registered companies is imposed, for the benefit of the national retirement fund.

Sweden

(c) Withholding taxes

Payments to non-resident companies:

	General rate	Rate applied under UK double taxation agreement
Dividends	30%	NIL or 5%*
Interest	NIL	NIL
Royalties	NIL	NIL

*The NIL rate to companies owning at least 10% of voting power.

SWITZERLAND

The Swiss Confederation is composed of 26 cantons which are further sub-divided into communes. Brief notes are also given hereunder on the taxes of the small Principality of Liechtenstein which adjoins and is closely associated with Switzerland.

The tax system of Switzerland is complicated by the multiplicity and interaction of the separate federal, cantonal and communal taxes on income and capital. In computing taxable income, the principle of "territoriality" is applied, so that income derived from a permanent establishment or real property outside Switzerland is not assessed for Swiss taxes. Similar principles are applied to concerns operating in more than one canton in the country, in order to ensure that a particular source of income is only taxed in one canton. For the taxation of companies and other legal entities, taxes paid are deductible in arriving at taxable income for federal taxation and this also applies to the computation in some cantons, but not in others. For individuals, the taxes paid do not reduce taxable income.

It is impossible in a brief summary of this nature to give a comprehensive statement of all the regulations and rates which apply in the various cantons, but an indication is given of the general form of the regulations and of the range of the rates of tax. The federal taxes, which are uniform throughout the country, represent a smaller part of the total tax burden than the cantonal and communal taxes, both for individuals and companies.

The rates of personal taxation are on average on fairly steeply progressive scales, bearing in mind that the rates quoted are often not for successive slices of taxable income but are increasing rates which apply to total taxable income.

The system of taxation of companies is such as to provide substantial tax benefits to holding companies set up in Switzerland whose income is derived from investments in other companies in which at least 20% of the equity is held. There is particularly favourable treatment of such companies in Liechtenstein. Switzerland has double taxation agreements with many countries and a careful watch is kept to ensure that the attractive benefits available are not abused, following a decree issued in 1962 designed to eliminate unjustified claims to take advantage of favourable tax rates.

There are modest wealth taxes on individuals and capital taxes on companies. Some kinds of capital gains accruing to individuals are not federally taxable but may be subject to cantonal taxes whose incidence varies.

1 LIST OF TAXES

(a) Federal Direct Tax (or Federal Defence Tax):
levied by the Federal authorities, through the medium of the cantonal tax administrations, on the income or profits of individuals and companies.

(b) Anticipatory Tax:
a Federal withholding tax deducted from dividend distributions and certain interest payments.

(c) Federal Capital Tax:
levied by the Federal authorities on the capital of companies. Capital for this purpose is shareholders' equity plus certain allocations to reserves which are not allowed as deductions in the income tax computation. The rate of tax is 0.0825%. (This tax is not further dealt with in this summary.)

(d) Cantonal and Communal taxes:
levied by each of the 26 Cantons and also by individual Communes, usually as a percentage of the taxes of the Canton.

    (i) Income taxes:
    levied on the income or profits of individuals and companies.

    (ii) Capital taxes:
    levied, like the Federal Capital Tax, on the capital of companies. Rates vary and the combined Federal, Cantonal and Communal rate ranges from about 0.4% to 1.3%: in Liechtenstein the normal rate is 0.2%. (These taxes are not further dealt with in this summary.)

    (iii) Wealth taxes:
    levied on the capital of individuals at rates varying between about 0.4% and 1.15%: in Liechtenstein the basic rate is 0.1%. (These taxes are not further dealt with in this summary.)

The Principality of Liechtenstein is closely associated with Switzerland and has a similar taxation system. Brief notes on this are given where appropriate.

2 INDIVIDUALS' INCOME TAXES

(a) Income charged (Federal, cantonal and communal taxes)
Residents: total world income, other than from real property or a permanent business establishment situated abroad.

Non-residents: Income derived from real property or a business, profession or employment in Switzerland. In addition, Anticipatory Tax is withheld from dividend and interest payments, and some cantons withhold tax from salaries and directors' fees paid to non-residents.

Any income which is not subject to tax in Switzerland (e.g. from real property abroad) is taken into account as part of total income for the purpose of determining the rates of tax payable on taxable income.

(b) Year and basis of assessment (Federal, cantonal and communal taxes)
The tax year is the calendar year or, for a business, its accounting year ending in the calendar year. The computation period used for tax purposes by the Federal authorities and most of the cantons covers two consecutive calendar years while the others use a one year period. The assessment period is one or two years, as the case may be, and tax is levied on the basis of the immediately preceding computation period. Where the assessment period covers two years, the tax for each year is based on the average taxable income of the two year computation period, and where it covers one year the tax is based on the taxable income of the one year computation period.

(c) Computation of taxable income
Taxable income is gross income less ordinary and necessary expenses and after deducting any personal allowances and any losses brought forward. There are differing tax regulations in the various cantons but, while rates of tax vary, in most respects the method of computation is the same for federal, cantonal and communal taxes. For individuals (unlike companies etc.) other taxes paid are not treated as deductible expenses. Cantonal tax authorities have the power to make tax assessments based on external evidence of wealth in cases where the tax return submitted is clearly erroneous. Resident foreigners with no Swiss earned income may elect

to be assessed for Federal tax on a notional income based on their living expenses.

Married couples and their dependent children are normally jointly assessed. Members of ordinary partnerships are individually liable for tax on their shares of profits, but limited partnerships with share capital are treated as companies.

(i) Business or professional income:
Basis
All proper business expenses are deductible in arriving at taxable income. Provisions and allocations to reserves for contingent liabilities are in many cases allowable deductions. Some cantons give relief for periods of up to 10 years from cantonal taxation for new manufacturing operations set up. Losses for Federal Direct Tax purposes incurred but unrecovered in one computation period may be carried forward for 7 years: there is varying treatment of losses for cantonal tax purposes.
Depreciation allowances
Basic rates of depreciation allowed are laid down for various categories of fixed asset other than land, to be applied on declining balance methods. Depreciation allowed for tax may not exceed the book depreciation.

(ii) Capital gains
Capital gains on disposal of business assets are taxable as ordinary business income. All gains on disposal of personal movable assets are exempt from federal tax but are taxed in some cantons and all cantons (as well as Liechtenstein) tax gains on disposal of real property, the rates varying widely.

(iii) Special trades
The only special provisions relate to such matters as air transport under double taxation agreements.

(iv) Salaries, wages etc., pensions
All kinds of income from employment and former employment derived from Switzerland are taxable, but taxable retirement income may be subject to a deduction of 40% or 20% if it arises under a contract wholly or partly paid for by the recipient.

For federal tax purposes, employees may deduct, within specified limits, certain costs such as travelling from home to office and meals away from home.

Tax at 30% is normally withheld from pensions etc., but the rate may be reduced, if the tax authorities approve, to 15% for pensions and 8% for other insurance benefits. Some cantons impose a final withholding tax on the earnings of transitory non-residents, such as actors or sportsmen, or on fees paid to non-resident directors: this covers both the federal and cantonal tax liability.

(v) Dividends, interest etc.

A withholding tax known as Anticipatory Tax at 35% (subject to the effect of double taxation agreements) is deductible from dividends and bond interest paid by Swiss companies, from payments of bank interest and from lottery winnings. Credit for the tax suffered is given to residents against their total tax liability. In Liechtenstein, the only withholding tax is a 4% coupon tax on dividends and bond interest.

(vi) Income from letting and leasing

Rental income from property in Switzerland and the rental value of owner-occupied property are included in taxable income.

(vii) Other income

All forms of income are taxable, including for instance royalties: there is no withholding tax on royalties.

(d) Deductions from total income (Federal, cantonal and communal taxes)

(i) General deductions

Deductions up to an overall total of 3,000F for married couples and 2,500F for others may be made for life or health insurance premiums, pension contributions and for interest received on savings.

(ii) Personal and other allowances

Personal allowances are given to married couples and there are allowances for children and other dependants.

(iii) Tax credits
Credit against the total liability is given for tax suffered by deduction at source, as well as any credits due under the provisions of double taxation agreements.

(e) Tax deducted at source
(i) Employment income   See (c) (iv) above.
(ii) Dividends, interest etc.   See (c) (v) above.

3 COMPANIES' TAXATION

(a) Types of undertaking charged
Public limited companies *(Aktiengesellschaften, "AG", or Sociétés anonymes, "SA")*
Private limited companies *("GmbH" or "SARL")*
Limited partnerships with shares
Foreign companies
Co-operatives

(b) Income charged (Federal, cantonal and communal taxes)
Resident companies etc. (i.e. those incorporated or registered in Switzerland): Total world income, other than from real property or a permanent establishment situated abroad.
Non-resident companies etc. (i.e. foreign companies): Income derived from real property or from a permanent establishment in Switzerland (liable for income taxes) and net assets in Switzerland (liable for capital taxes).

(c) Computation of taxable income (Federal, cantonal and communal taxes)
The computation of taxable income is in the main in accordance with the same rules as for individuals, so far as applicable. Particular points to be noted are:

(i) An important difference from the taxation of individuals is that, in computing income for the purposes of federal tax (and for taxes in about half of the cantons), taxes paid on income and capital are admissible deductions.

(ii) Realised capital gains are in most cases treated in the same way as trading income.

(iii) Dividends received by a resident company from another company (either Swiss or foreign) in which it has a substantial interest (i.e. 20% of the equity or a value for tax purposes exceeding 2 million francs) are subject to federal tax at a rate reduced in the same proportion as that of the dividends to the total gross income of the company. A holding company whose income consists wholly of dividends qualifying as above can therefore claim a refund of all anticipatory tax deducted from the dividends. Income from a permanent establishment abroad is in any case exempt (see (b) above), but this further exemption applies also where there is no such establishment. Similar, though in some cases more restricted, exemptions are given under most of the cantonal tax laws.

(iv) Some cantons give special tax privileges (which do not apply to federal tax) to "domiciliary" companies (i.e. those with only a registered office in Switzerland and with no personnel other than directors and no business activities in Switzerland) and to "mixed" or "auxiliary" companies ("domiciliary" companies with some extension of functions). Special rulings as to federal taxation apply to "service" companies (i.e. foreign-controlled Swiss companies which provide services to related foreign companies) under which they are treated as having a minimum taxable income based on a proportion of their expenses or payroll costs.

(v) In addition to the federal and cantonal capital taxes (see 1.(c) and (d) above) there is the federal defence tax on income, the rate of which depends on the percentage of taxable income on the capital of the company, rising to a maximum rate where income exceeds 23% of capital. The regulations for the taxing of income and the rates applied in the different cantons vary considerably, some using a computation similar to that for federal tax and others merely applying graduated rates to taxable income: some information on the rates is shown at 5. below.

4 DOUBLE TAXATION

Comprehensive double taxation agreements are in force between Switzerland and the United Kingdom and also about 25 other countries: in addition, the UK agreement has been extended to about 15 formerly dependent territories. Liechtenstein has no such agreements except with Austria, and residents of the Principality are liable to double taxation on income from abroad (e.g. from Switzerland).

5 RATES OF TAX

The rates of tax are subject to change from year to year, but the sample figures shown below for 1983 give an indication of recent rates. Amounts are stated in Swiss francs (F). Liechtenstein rates are shown separately.

(a) Individuals

Federal Direct Tax rises on a graduated scale for different levels of taxable income after 10,600F (up to which no tax is payable), reaching a maximum of 11.5% on total taxable income of over 392,900F. There are personal allowances of 4,000F for married couples and 2,000F for each child or other dependant and, if both spouses are working, up to 4,000F of the one with the lower income is tax-free.

For the combined total of cantonal and communal rates of tax, the maximum figures reached at the stated levels of taxable income (which in most cases are lower than the 392,900F for Federal Direct Tax) range from about 13% to about 40%. In most cases there is no lower exemption limit for taxable incomes. Personal allowances are given, sometimes higher than those for federal tax.

(b) Companies etc.

The maximum rate of Federal Direct Tax is 9.8% on taxable income where this shows a yield on capital of over 23%, with lower rates on smaller yields.

The effective rates of cantonal and communal taxes depend on whether or not, in a particular canton, taxes paid are deductible in arriving at taxable income. Taking this into account, the combined maximum rates of federal, cantonal and communal taxation on income range from about 20% to about 40%.

(c) Withholding taxes

Payments to non-resident companies:

Switzerland

	General rate	Rate applied under UK double taxation agreement
Dividends	35%	15% or 5%*
Interest		
(Bond and bank only)	35%	NIL
Royalties	NIL	NIL

*The lower rate to a company owning 25% or more of the voting power.

(d) Liechtenstein

Income tax of individuals reaches a maximum combined rate of about 20%.

For companies etc., the general rate of tax on taxable income varies between 7.5% and 15%, plus an addition of between 1% and 5% if dividends are distributed. Holding and "domiciliary" companies (see 3. (c) (iv) above) are however exempt from corporate income tax and only pay capital tax at 0.1% (with a minimum of 1,000F per annum).

UNITED KINGDOM

The income tax system of the United Kingdom has developed over many years during which it has been defined and refined by amending legislation and by case law. The system was reorganised and modernised by the introduction of a classical system of corporation tax in 1964, which was changed to an imputation system in 1973, and by the commencement of a capital gains tax in 1965. The introduction of value added tax (VAT) in 1973 made it possible to reduce or hold down the rates of direct taxation on income and gains.

In 1973/74, when a graduated scale of income tax was adopted instead of a standard rate of income tax with a separate surtax on higher incomes, the previous earned income allowance ceased and an investment income surcharge was introduced. The latter has continued until 1983/84 but has now ceased. The taxation of individuals is on a progressive scale, but this has been considerably less steep since 1979/80 due to changes in the scale and the removal of the very high rates which previously applied to taxable income over £14,000. The impact of the capital gains tax has also been modified since it was first introduced, both by the cessation of the separate taxation of short-term capital gains and by the raising of the exemption limits for the lower levels of gains and disposals. In order to deal with changing circumstances, caused by continuing inflation, provision has been made in recent years for the amounts of various reliefs, exemptions etc. to be altered annually in proportion to price levels under an 'indexation' system.

The taxation of businesses and, in particular, of companies was modified by the withdrawal in 1966 of investment allowances on qualifying capital expenditure and the introduction of free depreciation (i.e. up to 100% in the first year) on plant and machinery. Investment grants, which had been given since 1966 in respect of certain types of capital expenditure, ceased in 1970, but regional development grants were introduced in 1972, as an incentive to capital development in less developed areas – these cover large parts of the United Kingdom outside S.E. England. The inception of "stock relief" in 1975, based on increases in the book amount of trading stock during an accounting year, provided some help to businesses over the problems arising from inflation.

A package of radical changes in business taxation over the next few years was announced in the March 1984 Budget Statement. These include the phased reduction of the standard rate of corporation tax from 52% to 35%, offset by the abolition of "stock relief" (less necessary with the reduced rate of inflation) and the phasing out of 100% free depreciation on plant and machinery and the high initial allowances on industrial buildings. These changes are estimated to result in a significant reduction in the overall burden of tax.

Foreigners resident in the United Kingdom for a tax year qualify for the same personal reliefs as UK nationals. There has also been a special concession whereby, if they retain a legal domicile outside the UK and are working for a foreign employer, they have been assessed to income tax on only 50% or 75% of their emoluments, but this special arrangement is being phased out, starting in 1984/85. Residents who are neither domiciled nor "ordinarily resident" in the UK pay tax in respect of most types of income only on amounts remitted to the UK. There are also special reliefs for UK residents on the emoluments of employment whose duties are carried out abroad, but this type of concession is being withdrawn except for absences of a year or more. Double taxation agreements are in force with a large number of other countries, and a form of unilateral relief is available to UK residents for taxation on foreign income which is not relieved by tax treaties.

The tax system of the United Kingdom does not apply to the Channel Islands or the Isle of Man which have their own separate regulations, though these have similarities with those which are applicable in the United Kingdom.

1 LIST OF TAXES AND LEGISLATION

The basic law relating to income tax and corporation tax is contained in the Income and Corporation Taxes Act 1970, as subsequently amended: the rates of tax are fixed by the Finance Acts which are passed at least once a year. The Capital Gains Tax Act 1979 consolidated the previous legislation on that tax.

(a) Income tax:
   levied on the income of individuals.

(b) Corporation tax:
   levied on the income and capital gains of companies.

(c) Capital gains tax:
   levied on the capital gains of individuals.

(d) Taxes not further dealt with in this summary:

   (i) Capital transfer tax:
   levied on individuals in respect of transfers of property on death and gifts during life.

   (ii) Development land tax:
   levied in respect of certain gains on development of land and buildings.

2 TAXATION OF INDIVIDUALS

(a) Income charged
   Residents: In general, income and gains from all sources, but for persons not domiciled or not ordinarily resident in the United Kingdom the liability on most types of income is limited to tax on sums remitted to the UK.
   Non-residents: Income arising in the UK.
   Residence in the UK for a particular tax year may be established in more than one way, e.g. presence in the UK for 183 days or more of the year, habitual visits to the UK for substantial periods of time (i.e. averaging 3 months per year) or the presence in the UK for any length of time of a person who has accommodation available for his use there. A person may be resident for tax purposes in more than one country in a year.
   The domicile of a person may be his domicile of origin

(i.e. at birth) or a domicile of choice, established subsequently, and in some cases its establishment may be a highly technical matter: a person has only one legal domicile at a particular time. "Ordinary residence" may also be established in a number of different ways.

There is special tax treatment of foreign emoluments. Persons not domiciled in the UK but working in the UK for a foreign employer are at present assessed on only 50% of their emoluments or 75% for persons who have been resident in the UK for 9 of the preceding 10 years. There are also reliefs under certain conditions in respect of emoluments from employment for UK residents whose duties are carried out abroad. The March 1984 Finance Bill however contains proposals for phasing out both these kinds of relief, except for UK residents working abroad for a year or more.

(b) Year and basis of assessment

The tax year ends on April 5th. Profits from a business, profession etc. are assessed on the basis of its accounting year ending in the preceding tax year. Certain interest received without deduction of tax and income from overseas possessions are taxed on the basis of amounts arising in the preceding tax year. Otherwise assessments are in general on a current year basis.

Assessments on the income of individuals (other than capital gains) are raised under six separate "schedules" for the different types of income as follows:

Schedule	Source of income
A	Rents received
B	Occupation of woodlands on a commercial basis
C	Interest on Government stocks taxed at source
D Case I	Trades and businesses
II	Professions etc.
III	Untaxed interest received
IV	Overseas securities
V	Overseas possessions
VI	Sundry profits
E	Employments etc.

F   Dividends etc. from companies resident in the UK

(c) Computation of taxable income

There are different detailed rules for the computation of taxable income assessed under each of the separate schedules referred to above. Total income from all sources, subject to exemptions, less charges, personal reliefs and losses, is the taxable income, the rate of income tax being on a graduated scale: capital gains are treated separately.

Married persons living together are normally jointly assessed: separate assessments may be claimed, but the overall total of tax is not affected thereby except where both have substantial earned income, with a combined total of about £23,800 or more. A joint assessment to income tax is made on a partnership: taxable profits are apportioned between the partners but the total tax may, in case of default, be recovered from any partner.

(i) Business or professional income:
Basis

Assessments on the profits of trades or professions (under Sch.D Cases I and II respectively) are both computed on the same lines. Subject to special provisions for commencement or cessation of a business, net taxable income of the accounting period ending within the preceding tax year is assessable. Admissible deductions in arriving at net taxable income include only those expenses incurred wholly and exclusively for the purpose of the business etc., and there are numerous provisions dealing with the allowability of different types of expense apart from that criterion. Premiums or contributions, within specified limits, paid by a self-employed person under an approved retirement benefit scheme are deductible in the assessment of earned income. Losses may be set off against other income of the year or carried forward for set-off against future profits of the same business.

Special relief is given as a deduction from taxable income for increases in trading stock calculated by reference to a special index of price levels, known as the "all stocks index". Charges for recovery of past relief may be made in certain circumstances under the "clawback" provisions. Under the terms of the Finance Bill of March 1984 this relief will no longer be given for accounting periods starting after 13 March 1984.

A form of investment incentive, originally introduced by the Finance Act 1981, was replaced with widened scope and new regulations by the Business Expansion Scheme included in the Finance Act 1983. This scheme provides for relief from tax to an individual on amounts subscribed for shares in a new qualifying company for the purposes of a new qualifying trade, subject to various conditions. The relief is limited to subscriptions of not more than £40,000 a year between 6 April 1983 and 5 April 1987.

Taxable income is normally computed on an earnings basis, but for a profession assessed under Case II a cash basis may be approved.

Depreciation allowances
Capital allowances given as a deduction in arriving at taxable profit (in place of any charges for depreciation shown in the accounts) include:

Industrial buildings: initial allowance generally 75% (hotels 20%, buildings in "enterprise zones" and small workshops 100%) of expenditure in the year and writing-down allowance 4%.

Plant and machinery: first-year allowance 100% of capital expenditure (other than on passenger cars).

Scientific research: first-year allowance 100% of capital expenditure (including buildings and plant etc.).

Under the terms of the March 1984 Finance Bill certain of the above allowances are being phased out – see 5(d) below.

Special provisions apply to initial, first-year and writing-down allowances for a number of special types of asset, including agricultural buildings and works, mines and oil wells.

Regional development grants at 20% or 22% are granted for certain expenditure on buildings, plant etc.

in specified development areas. The grant does not reduce the amount on which capital allowances are calculated.

(ii) Capital gains

Subject to a number of exemptions, capital gains on disposal of assets by individuals are assessable to capital gains tax. Exemptions in the year 1983/84 include:

1. The first £5,300 of chargeable gains in a year.
2. Disposals of household goods, chattels etc. for £3,000 or less in a year.
3. British Government securities held for a year or more.
4. Private cars.
5. Subject to certain conditions, gains on disposal of a private residence.

For 1984/85 the March 1984 Finance Bill provided for an increase in the annual exemption of chargeable gains from £5,300 to £5,600 and for the exemption, similar to that for British Government securities, of gains on disposal of corporate loan stocks held for a year or more.

The rate of capital gains tax on chargeable gains is 30%.

(iii) Special trades

There are a number of special provisions applicable to particular types of business, as for instance in relation to farming (herd basis etc.), commercial woodlands (assessed under Sch.B), professions in general (e.g. use of cash, rather than earnings basis) and in relation to capital allowances on assets used in various trades. There are also a number of special rules, mainly applicable to corporation tax on companies, for particular types of business such as investment companies and investment trusts, life assurance companies, banks, building societies, friendly societies, industrial and provident societies and oil producers (liable for Petroleum Revenue Tax). There are restricted double taxation agreements with some countries applying only to shipping and air transport.

(iv) Salaries, wages etc., pensions

Income from employment and former employment is in general assessed under Sch.E but some pensions from abroad may come under Sch.D Case V. All emoluments and pensions and, in principle, all perquisites from employment are assessable as earned income. Subject to exemptions, the value of benefits provided by the employer is included in taxable emoluments: exemptions may include, *inter alia,* employers' payments for approved retirement benefit schemes, living accommodation provided for an employee who must occupy it for the proper performance of his duties, and luncheon vouchers or subsidised canteen facilities: in this connection, special provisions apply in some cases to benefits for directors and senior employees. Special provisions apply to charges for private use of a car supplied by an employer partly for business use.

An employee's own contributions to an approved retirement benefit scheme are deductible expenses. Admissible travelling expenses do not include the cost of travel from home to place of work. Other expenses are allowed only if wholly, exclusively and necessarily incurred in the performance of the duties of the employment.

Tax is deducted under a PAYE system from all salaries, wages etc.

For foreign emoluments see the reference at 2.(a) above.

(v) Dividends, interest etc.

A United Kingdom resident's income from dividends includes, in addition to the cash amount, a tax credit (equivalent to the advance corporation tax payable by the company making the distribution): for 1983/84 the tax credit is 3/7ths of the dividend or 30% of the dividend plus tax credit.

Tax is deducted at source from interest on most Government stocks and is collected from the paying agent under Sch.C. Interest on certain Government stocks is exempt from tax for non-residents.

Tax is in general deductible at source from annual interest paid by companies but not by individuals. Except for interest on home loans (since 1 April 1983), tax is not deducted from bank interest.

Dividends and interest are included in the income which is liable to the investment income surcharge (see 5.(a) (ii) below).

(vi) Income from letting and leasing

Property rents receivable, less the cost of maintenance, repairs and other expenses, are assessable under Sch.A. There is no charge for tax on the annual value of an owner-occupied property. Tax is deductible at source from rents only when paid to a non-resident. Rents form part of the income which is liable to the investment income surcharge.

(vii) Sundry income

Tax is deductible at source from patent royalties and from copyright royalties paid to non-residents. Lump sums received on assignment of copyrights may be spread retrospectively over the years (up to three) occupied in producing the work. Other miscellaneous income, such as that from furnished lettings, is assessable under Sch.D Case VI.

(d) Deductions from total income

(i) General deductions

Admissible deductions include annuities, payments under deeds of covenant etc. (payable less tax) and interest payable on certain loans: on a loan for the purchase or improvement of the borrower's main residence, interest is an admissible deduction but with a limit of interest on £30,000.

(ii) Personal and other allowances

Personal reliefs include married and single allowances, wife's earned income allowance and allowances for age and for certain dependants. Relief for life assurance premiums is now given by a deduction of 15% from premiums paid. These reliefs are allowed only to United Kingdom residents (including foreigners) except that British subjects and a few other special categories resident abroad are entitled to partial relief in the same proportion as that of their UK income to their world income.

(iii) Tax credits
Relief is given for tax suffered by deduction at source, for the tax credit under the imputation system on dividends received (see (c) (v) above) and for any credits due under double taxation agreements or under arrangements for unilateral relief against double taxation.

(e) Tax deducted at source
(i) Employment income See (c) (iv) above.
(ii) Interest   See (c) (v) above.
(iii) Rents   See (c) (vi) above re non-residents.
(iv) Royalties   See (c) (vii) above re non-residents.

3 CORPORATION TAX

(a) Types of undertaking charged
A "company" chargeable to corporation tax is any body corporate or unincorporated association: this definition does not include partnerships or local authorities.

(b) Income charged
Resident companies (i.e. those whose central management and control are in the United Kingdom): Profits from all sources.
Non-resident companies: Profits arising from a branch or agency in the United Kingdom.

(c) Computation of taxable income
An "imputation system" of corporation tax was adopted in 1973. Under this system, a company paying a dividend or making any other qualifying distribution pays "advance corporation tax" (ACT), at 3/7ths of the dividend, etc., which is offset against the company's "mainstream" corporation tax liability: any surplus ACT may be surrendered to, and used by, a subsidiary, or may be carried backward for up to two years to an earlier accounting period, or may be carried forward indefinitely: in the hands of the recipient of the distribution, the gross amount to be included in his total taxable income is the actual cash received plus a tax credit equivalent to the ACT (see 2.(c) (v) above).
The profits of a company are computed on the basis of its accounting periods and apportioned over financial years which, for this purpose, end on March 31st. In general (but

with some exceptions) profits chargeable to corporation tax are computed in accordance with the same rules as for income tax payable by an individual, so far as applicable. Chargeable capital gains, computed as for capital gains tax charged on an individual, but without the annual £5,300 exemption, are included in profits subject to corporation tax, but are charged at an effective rate of 30%. Profits for corporation tax purposes do not include any distributions received from companies resident in the United Kingdom: these distributions, in the hands of the recipient company, are known as "franked investment income" and the tax credit applicable to the income may be used to offset the ACT on its own qualifying distributions or, in some circumstances, payment of the tax credit may be claimed.

"Group relief" is available in groups of United Kingdom resident companies and is effective between a holding company and a 75% subsidiary or between two 75% subsidiaries and also between members of a consortium, whereby relief for trading losses may be surrendered by one company and used by a claimant company to offset taxable profits.

Special provisions apply to building societies, housing associations, industrial and provident societies, investment trusts, life assurance companies and unit trusts. Revenue from oil production in the United Kingdom or the continental shelf is subject to Petroleum Revenue Tax, currently at 75%, under special regulations.

"Close companies", as defined, are subject to a number of restrictions and special provisions, and in certain circumstances undistributed income may be apportioned to participators (shareholders and others with an interest as defined) as taxable income.

4   DOUBLE TAXATION

Comprehensive double taxation agreements are in force between the United Kingdom and over 70 other countries, including a large number of former colonies and dependencies, as well as a number of agreements confined to shipping and air transport matters. A form of unilateral relief is also given to United Kingdom residents for foreign tax on income arising abroad which is also subject to UK tax.

5 RATES OF TAX

Rates of tax are subject to change from year to year but the sample figures shown below, dealing with income tax for the year 1983/84 and corporation tax for the year from 1 April 1982, are instances of recent rates. Amounts are stated in pounds sterling (£).

(a) Income tax

(i) A basic rate of 30% applies to the first £14,600 of taxable income: higher rates apply to subsequent slices of taxable income, rising to 60% on the excess over £36,000.

(ii) An investment income surcharge of 15% is levied additionally on all taxable income, other than earned income, after the first £7,100.

(iii) Personal reliefs, for some of which annual changes in amount are normally linked to changes in the retail price index, include:

Personal allowance: single   £1,785
                married   £2,795
Wife's earned income relief   100% (up to a maximum of £1,785)
Age allowance: single   £2,360   (income limit
              married   £3,755   £7,600)

There are also allowances for certain dependants but no longer for children except, in certain cases, for children living abroad or students over 19 for whom child benefit allowance is not payable.

(b) Corporation tax

(i) The full rate of corporation tax is 52% for the financial year 1982 (commencing 1 April 1982). There is a reduced rate of 38% for small companies, i.e. those whose taxable profits do not exceed £100,000 (with marginal relief up to £500,000).

(ii) The rate of advance corporation tax for the financial year 1983 (commencing 1 April 1983) is 3/7th or 30% of the cash distribution plus the related tax credit.

(c) *Withholding taxes*

Subject to the effect of any double taxation agreement, tax deducted from payments of interest, royalties or rents is at the basic rate of 30%.

(d) *Budget proposals 1984/85*

In the March 1984 Finance Bill (now an Act) no change was proposed in the basic 30% rate of income tax but the threshold for the higher rates is increased from £14,600 to £15,400 and, after changes in the other higher rate bands, the top rate of 60% is to be reached at the excess over £38,100 instead of £36,000. Both the investment income surcharge and life assurance relief on new policies are abolished. The indexation of personal reliefs was again suspended but increases in personal allowances (larger than under the indexation provisions) are given to £2,005 (single) and £3,155 (married) and there are comparable increases in other reliefs. Increases in exemptions for capital gains tax are mentioned at 2(c)(ii) above.

Widespread changes in corporation tax provisions were announced. The standard rate is reduced to 50% for 1983 and further reductions are intended to 45% for 1984, 40% for 1985 and 35% for 1986: the small companies rate is reduced to 30% for 1983 and future years. However, stock relief (see 2(c)(i) above) is abolished for periods starting after 13 March 1984 and, under the heading of capital allowances, the 100% first-year allowance for plant and machinery is reduced to 75% and both this and the 75% initial allowance for industrial buildings are to be phased out by 1986.

DATE DUE

GAYLORD			PRINTED IN U.S.A.